Dream Culture, Bringing Dreams to Life is
to partner with God for the impossible. 1.
to have fulfilled dreams in our efforts to honor the Lord through every
part of our lives. Andy and Janine Mason take the reader on a journey
through mind-stretching exercises that build hope while helping to define
our purpose. This book not only shows us how to dream, it awakens us
to our responsibility to live towards the impossible. Rare is the book that
is so intensely practical yet so powerfully supernatural. *Dream Culture*
embodies both beautifully. I look forward to seeing the affect this book
will have on the hearts and minds of believers around the world.

Bill Johnson
Senior Leader, Bethel Church, Redding California
Author, *When Heaven Invades Earth* and *The Essential Guide to Healing*
www.BJM.org

Andy and Janine Mason bring a profound workbook and tool that is one
part life coach, one part counselor, and a major direction builder in your
relationship to your life and destiny. I read the book three times the first
month I got it and it changed the way I minister to people because of its
insight. Anyone who is in transition or in need of greater direction or
doesn't have specific ideas of how to pursue dreams should read this book.
It will really help you journey through a deliberate process of thinking
that is both biblical based and inspirationally triggered. I give this book
my highest recommendation for the subject.

Shawn Bolz
Senior Pastor, Expression58, Los Angeles California
Author, *Keys To Heaven's Economy* and *The Nonreligious Guide to Dating*
www.Expression58.org

Your revitalized dreams are the flash-point for an ever-growing, wonder-
filled life. The first step is to know that your dreams and God's will are
on the same page and then to follow proven pathways. Andy and Janine
are your personal, Life Dream Sherpas that guide you along the journey.
Dream Culture simplifies your process and empowers you for success.
Team Mason lives the dream every day and is a great, ongoing source
of inspiration to our entire team. We thank them for their character and
their anointed work.

Rick Sbrocca
Founder, Spiritus Solutions

Living in a Dream Culture is learning to partner with God's hopes for your life. I have witnessed this first in our middle school. Through the introduction of the principles in this book to our students I have watched hope arise. Our middle school has experienced a truly positive culture shift. This Dream Culture released our students to set their sights high, celebrate others' dreams, and be a positive influence to those around them. I highly recommend this book to those that want to partner with God.

H. Don Mayer
Principal, Bethel Christian School, Redding, California
www.BCSRedding.org

Surveys show that nearly eighty-five percent of Christians live passive, unfulfilled lives. That's about to change! *Dream Culture* by Andy and Janine is a transformational dream coaching tool to help you release the dream God has placed in your heart. As a dreamer, everything I need is in this book to help me become a greater history-maker and world-changer."

Leif Hetland
Founder and President, Global Mission Awareness
Author, *Seeing Through Heaven's Eyes*
www.GlobalMissionAwareness.com

As a powerful last days tool, *Dream Culture* teaches you how to put feet to your dreams, positions and equips you to literally walk them out with character, intentionality, effectiveness and victory! I love the supernatural aspect of all the amazing testimonies of God intervening and making the dreams He's put within people a tangible reality. This is a book that will activate hope and if you and your dreams have fallen off the hope train; here is your ticket back on!

Lori Byrne
Co-Founder, Love After Marriage Workshops
www.LoveAfterMarriage.org

Dream Culture will push you out of religious boxes to encounter God as He really is--the Father that loves your dreams and wants to meet you in them. Hang around with Andy and Janine, and every day you'll hear a new testimony of how someone's dream came true--and how that individual met God and got to know a new side of Him in the process.

If you want to understand hope, and how God delights in our smallest desires, these two embody it.

Tony Stoltzfus
Certified Professional Coach Trainer
Author, *Leadership Coaching* and *Coaching Questions*
www.Coach22.com

We always say to our clients, "Don't die wondering what might have been possible. Step out and have a red hot go!" This timely book opens up your heart and mind to what God has on offer for you, and gives you practical strategies for getting the rubber on the road. *Dream Culture* needs to be in your personal toolbox. Buy a copy for your best friend as well.

Steve & Tara Connell
Kingdom Business Builders, New Zealand
www.KingdomBusinessBuilders.com

Andy and Janine Mason's *Dream Culture* is a catalytic book to help people understand what their dreams are, what is hindering their fulfillment and what is needed to live the "dream life" that God has ordained for each one of us. The whole book is great, but the dream activity questions at the end of each chapter are worth the price of the book alone. This is a must read for those who desire to reach their full potential in life."

Steve Backlund
Founder and President, Ignited Hope
Author, *Victorious Mindsets* and *Cracks in the Foundation*
www.IgnitedHope.com

Andrew and Janine have written an outstanding book that will be a real help towards the fulfillment of many people's dreams! Do you want to actually live your dreams? Then read this book and put it into practice. Many writers and speakers have set out to encourage and inspire people to dream but there are few who have been able to articulate the "how" – the Mason's have gone the extra mile by showing us the "how." This book is intensely personal and practical. On a personal note, one question from the author propelled me towards the fulfillment of a lifetime dream and adventure. For this I am forever grateful.

Lao Da Ge
Pastor, China

Dreams are not about unreal expectations or only faith driven desires. Without them our life is senseless, lacking purpose, reduced only to routine and control. God has given a dream to each of us since He created us. Living and dreaming imply risk and there is no safety net when we jump. We do not know all that is along the way or at the end, but God knows because He is already there. In *Dream Culture*, Andy and Janine dig into this risk taking area of purposeful living. God wants us to leave our comfort zone's to make a difference. Andy and Janine are aligned with God's purpose of building a community of dreamers, a new culture, where dreams can be achieved one step at a time, recovering the joy of life and sense of purpose. This book is an important seed in a new field of unleashing the power of people's dreams.

Juan Carlos Flores Zuniga
President and Co-founder, Liderinnova Foundation, Costa Rica

Dream Culture is a game-changer. It will undoubtedly assist you in fulfilling your life's dreams. This treasure tool can free you to realize more of your God-given potential, and embark you on a journey of living your dream with the nurture and affirmation of a supportive culture. Dream discovery and realization happens in community with those who share your dream--with those people who see more in you than you can see in yourself. Andy and Janine model living their dream, and with *Dream Culture*, provide you with a world class vehicle that is sure to become a classic.

Robert 'Bud' Hancock
Founder and Chairman, Providence International Foundation
www.ProvidenceInternational.org

This book totally changed the trajectory of our lives. My wife, Robbie, attended a Dream Culture presentation and received coaching from Janine. After 33 years of marriage and my involvement in business, Robbie fulfilled her dream of becoming my business partner. This book not only changed our marriage and our business, but it also brought us into a deeper level of covenant in marriage. Dare to be a dreamer!

Mike Frank
Founder, Frank Consulting
Author, *Prosperity with a Purpose*
www.Mikefrankconsulting.com

At last there is a book that practically helps us to not only dream, but gives us helpful steps in how to achieve those dreams. I found the questions at the end of each chapter especially helpful, as well as the coaching aspect, which allows us to take ownership and responsibility in taking actions steps toward their fulfillment. One of the greatest motivators in this book has to be 'why' dreams are so important for us to cultivate and what could be keeping us back from fulfilling them. If you want to hear testimonies about people living their dreams and how the quality of their life has improved - you've got to read this book! As I read this book, I couldn't put it down, because it made me realize the time is NOW to fulfill my dreams. Don't wait! Get this book today, and find out how you can see your dreams become a reality!

Theresa Dedmon
Creative Arts Director, Bethel Church, Redding California
www.TheresaDedmonMinistries.com

FOREWARD BY DANNY SILK

D.REAM
culture
bringing dreams to life

ANDY & JANINE MASON

DREAM
culture
Bringing Dreams to Life

©2011 Andy and Janine Mason
All rights reserved.

Cover design, book design & formatting by Lorraine Box:
propheticart@sbcglobal.net

Authors' photo by Firefly Mobile Studio:
www.firefly2u.com

ISBN-13: 978-1456361419
ISBN-10:1456361414

To order more books or to learn more about the authors,
please visit the authors' website:
www.idreamculture.com

Printed in the United States of America

CONTENTS

TESTIMONIES

ACKNOWLEDGMENTS

Danny Silk. *Thanks for showing me what freedom looks like and trusting in me more than I trust in myself! Thanks for living this message and inspiring others to do the same. You have been the catalyst for a Global Dream Culture.*

Charlie Harper & Tony Stoltzfus. *Thank you for being the sounding board of wisdom, patience and experience that turns a good idea into a great plan.*

Jason Hedge & Ana Cho. *Thanks for starting the Dreamvesting Program at Bethel Church and then graciously passing that initial momentum on to us. Thank you for your encouragement and advice.*

Anne Kalvestrand. *You are a lifeline of hope. Your friendship has smeared us with favor and encouragement that money could never buy. Thank you for making our family yours.*

Lorraine Box. *Your love and belief in us has meant the world. Thank you for translating that belief into hours of work that has made this project a beautiful thing. You rock!*

Robert & Mary Sutherland. *You have been a gift of God to us like an impact player in the final quarter of the Super Bowl. At a critical stage you entered our world and ensured that our efforts paid off. We are in awe of your contribution. Thank you.*

Steve & Tara Connell. *Your insights around sharpening our activations have been invaluable. Thanks for your encouragement and friendship.*

Our Dream Coaches at Bethel Church. *Thank you for your patience as we have learned together. Thanks for committing your lives to build a Dream Culture and see the dreams of others become reality.*

FOREWORD

It's hard to imagine that all of this started in a Chinese restaurant in downtown Redding, California. I thought I was meeting with Andy to help him figure out a place to somehow happen at Bethel Church. He thought he was meeting to help me, possibly as an intern. We had no way of knowing that we would be building our lives together for decades to come.

The first major paradox came when he informed me that he felt that he was supposed to offer his services as my intern. But he then launched into an explanation of not being interested in anything I was leading in: *"I don't want to do any counseling or really have much to do with Family Life. I'm not really interested in pastoring or outreach, so I'm not sure how I would intern for you,"* he said. My role at Bethel Church at this time was the Family Life Pastor.

I continued listening as he fumbled around, seeming to search for the meaning of this lunchtime connection. He was an unknown to me up to this point. I was shocked by his New Zealand (Kiwi) accent and had no idea what he'd done for a living prior to uprooting his wife and four small children and moving to California. I began to ask questions of this interesting Kiwi. I soon found out that he was as deep as he was bright. He had been a Relationship Manager for a bank in New Zealand, an agricultural business consultant and a shepherd on a large training ranch. He carried a wide range of experiences for a Kiwi, from sheep and cattle ranching to banking. However, his role as a

Relationship Manager is what caught my attention.

As a Relationship Manager at the bank, Andy's role was to interview sheep and cattle ranchers and inquire about their long-term vision for their business and family. In doing so, he would be invited into their dreams of accomplishment, retirement and succession planning. He had no idea who he was talking to at this moment and I had no idea who had just walked into my life.

In searching about who Andy was, where he was from and what he had done up to this point in his life, I discovered a man with a huge, passionate and energetic heart. His heart includes the rebirth of a fathering movement on the earth in this generation. His vision is much more than helping shepherds find their way. He told me of his desire to see successive generations of fathers arise who would activate those around them to discover purpose and empower them to live it well. As we spoke I began to feel a deep connection forming around this idea that fathers must take their rightful place in the lives of those around them; a place of hope, strength and encouragement. Our little Chinese lunch was beginning to spawn a vision that ultimately led to my role change at Bethel. Our conversation was tapping into my dream.

Meanwhile, and unknown to Andy, several of our team were experimenting with and developing what we initially called *Dreamvesting* at Bethel Church. Borrowing inspiration from a book called *The Dream Manager* by Matthew Kelly, we were determined to create an environment where people could see their dreams coming true in the context of a supportive work environment. Our program was progressing, but slow-going because the work was being done by those who had other pressing responsibilities. I had an idea ...

Andy and Janine went to work on a yearlong internship launching *Dreamvesting* into hyperspace. They immediately began building a team of Dream Coaches and started a training process to bring them along quickly and effectively. By the end of the first year they had a growing team of over 20 Dream Coaches and had opened up the dreams of well over 100 of our people. Word spread fast that a major infusion of hope was available through this program. Soon Janine kicked in as the primary director and trainer in *Dreamvesting*. Her leadership is what keeps this opportunity flourishing at Bethel today.

The name changed to *Dream Culture* because we truly believe this is the vision. We want a culture that supports people at every level to fulfill their God given destiny. This material is now a training template for us to inspire others in hope, strength and courage toward their dreams. Andy and Janine unpack and lay out what can be a complex process, in numerous, but simple steps.

I have spent much of my life bringing hope and healing to broken lives, marriages and relationships. I am so excited about what Andy and Janine are bringing because it is a set of tools and paradigms to help people who need motivation, other than pain, for change, vision and purpose. Great things happen in people when they find their dreams can become a reality. We've all known some type of experience with "hope deferred," but to know a process of realizing our dreams is truly a "tree of life." Please enjoy and flourish as you learn and apply Dream Culture to your life and that of your environment.

Peace,

Danny Silk

Staff & Leadership Development Director, Bethel Church
Author of *Culture of Honor* and *Loving Our Kids on Purpose*

*When the LORD brought
back the captivity of Zion,
We were like those who
dream.*

*Then our mouth was
filled with laughter,
And our tongue with singing.*

*Then they said
among the nations,
"The LORD has done great
things for them."*

Psalm 126:1,2

A group of six-year-olds was in a drawing class
with their elementary school teacher.
One little girl sat at the back of the class.
With arms curled around her paper, she was totally absorbed in
what she was doing for more than twenty minutes.
The teacher found this fascinating.
Eventually, she asked the girl what she was drawing.
Without looking up, the girl said,
"I'm drawing a picture of God."
Surprised, the teacher said,
"But nobody knows what God looks like."
The girl said,
"They will in a minute."

~ Adapted from *The Element*, by Dr Ken Robinson

The world is waiting to see what picture your life
paints of Who He is.

Live well.

Andy & Janine Mason

the dream
the invitation

God had a dream
and wrapped your body around it.

~ Lou Engle

a global dream culture

How would it feel to have someone not only believe in you and your dreams, but also work alongside you to help those dreams become reality? What would it be like if we lived in a community where everyone was intentionally seeking to encourage and empower one another to discover their purpose and live their dream? We believe that kind of community is possible and it starts with you and me. So, what is your dream and how can we help you live it well?

Our dream is to catalyze a *Global Dream Culture* where people everywhere join together in community to help one another succeed in life—life as God *made us* to live it. It's a culture full of courage to face the impossible, love that overcomes fear, and the tangible Presence and Power of God that make the supernatural a daily experience. It's a culture where people genuinely know and commit to help one another discover the gold God put in each of us—then to walk alongside each other to see the fullness of that gold expressed.

*Impossible
is just a big word
thrown around by small men
who find it easier to live in the
world
they've been given
than explore the power they have
to change it.
Impossible is not a fact.
It's an opinion.
Impossible is not a declaration.
It's a dare.
Impossible is potential.
Impossible is temporary.
Impossible is nothing.*

~ Adidas

In working with people all around us, we get the greatest reward seeing their lives transformed into who they were born to be. We have the privilege of partnering with people and seeing the joy of a dream realized or a victory celebrated in overcoming a dream barrier. As people begin to shine, no matter what they are made of, life is released that reminds us we really were made in the image of God. It is true as Saint Irenaeus was quoted as saying in 202 AD that *"the glory of God is a man fully alive."* If Christ came that we might have life and life to the *full*, then discovering and living your dreams is part of the process. All creation is groaning in anticipation of seeing you and the people around you *fully alive!*

an interactive dream journey

The purpose of this book is to unlock the dreams within you and unleash you to walk those dreams out to fulfillment. We live in the world we create with our words and actions. If you want to live a different future than your present circumstances reveal, then you will need to think differently, speak differently and act differently. The challenge is that all this involves change and change involves walking through the discomfort of doing things differently.

It is our hope that this book will be a catalyst and companion to you on that journey. It is designed to be interactive, so we encourage you to take the time to work through the Dream Activation Exercises that will turn your ideas into habits, then into a lifestyle of intentionally living your dreams.

> *Aim at Heaven and you will get earth thrown in.*
>
> *Aim at earth and you get neither.*
>
> ~ C. S. Lewis

setting you up to succeed

We encourage you to find a Dream Friend or Dream Partner as you begin this journey *(we will talk more on this in a later chapter)*. This is a person with whom you can share your journey and who will encourage you and hold you accountable to your dreams. Choose wisely, as many a person has had their dream crushed by a well-meaning friend whose intention was to save them from disappointment. It is amazing how God, who *is* love, encourages us to take risks beyond ourselves, but also promises He will never leave our side. He is the greatest Dream Partner of all!

are you ready?

So before we start this journey, we encourage you to take a moment to consider the adventure you are about to undertake. Your life is likely to be different by the time you finish this book and apply its principles to your life.

Are you ready to say *YES* to our Father in Heaven's invitation to pursue a life fully alive? Are you ready to let go of past disappointments, fears and failures and dream again? Are you ready to make conscious choices and take actions every day to move toward making those dreams a reality? Are you ready for your life to become an inspiration and an overflow of life and joy to those around you? If your answer to these questions is *YES*, then read on!

dream activation exercise

step one | **Reconnect With a Dream**

Take a few moments to close your eyes and think of a significant dream you achieved in the past. Maybe it was graduating from college, getting your driver's license or getting married…

— Let your thoughts go back to the details of achieving that dream.

— Put yourself back into that experience and allow yourself to relive the emotions.

— What sights, smells, sounds and sensations are you aware of when you experienced achieving that dream?

step two | **Reflect**

Now that you have reconnected with that dream, jot down some thoughts about it:

— How did you feel when you fulfilled that dream, or when you recalled it?

— Describe how achieving that dream impacted you. How did it affect you emotionally? How did it affect your motivation in other areas of your life?

— Now think about the people around you at the

time. How were they impacted by you achieving your dream?

— Now imagine the impact on your wider community of everyone living their dream.

From this exercise you will have reconnected with the life that is released in and around you on the Dream Journey. Use this to motivate you on your renewed journey of living your dreams!

what is a dream?

*A dream is a picture of the future
I want to live in someday.*

As we get started, it's important that we speak the same language. So when we refer to a *dream*, what are we talking about?

*Dreams are seeds of possibility planted in your soul,
calling you to pursue a unique path
to the realization of your purpose.*

~ John Maxwell, *Put Your Dream to the Test*

A dream is a picture of the future I want to live in someday. One of the most widely known dreamers of the twentieth century was Dr. Martin Luther King, Jr., remembered especially for his powerful and moving speech, *"I Have a Dream,"* delivered in 1963, on the steps of the Lincoln Memorial in Washington, D.C., to a crowd of more than 200,000. In this speech he articulated a picture of the future he wanted to live in, where his children would not be judged by the color of their skin, but by the content of their character; where black men, white men, Jews, Gentiles, Protestants and Catholics, would hold hands together and stand on the solid rock of brotherhood to make justice a reality for all of God's children, as was written into this nation's Constitution and Declaration of Independence. Martin Luther King, Jr., died in the pursuit of his dream, but his dream lives on in the lives of countless people who hold on to that same dream. As Tony Stoltzfus writes in his book, *A Leader's Life Purpose, "Dreams are powerful. Dreams and those who live them can change cultures, redirect nations and move mountains."*

Every great dream begins with a dreamer.

Always remember, you have within you the strength, the patience, and the passion to reach for the stars to change the world.

~ Harriet Tubman

Dreams are hope carriers and are not bound by time or present circumstances. On the other hand, goals are measurable, time specific and require more than just hope; they require action. This book is not intended to be just a broker of hope, but also to be a tool to combine action with hope, to put legs on people's dreams.

Martin Luther King, Jr. didn't just dream. He made very clear and concise steps to do everything within his power to make his dream a reality. He broke his dream down into goals that would put legs on that dream, and in doing so, he empowered others all around him to do the same.

So what are *your* dreams and what can *you* do to make them a reality?

THE POWER OF A DREAM

Joylyn (not her real name) grew up in a highly dysfunctional and abusive family. One thing led to another and she ended up in her early 30's as a single mother with three children. She was struggling with her children's anger at life, expressed in violence toward her. The cycle of dysfunction was repeating itself. The next outburst of anger with her oldest son resulted in Child Protection Services requiring her to take an anger management class or lose custody of her child. In the midst of this situation, she happened to attend a Dream Workshop at a local community center.

During the Dream Workshop, Joylyn had a revelation of what it means to be a child of God. Hope was released and she was unlocked to dream again. She started to write her re-discovered dreams but they could not be contained on one page and spilled over onto the next page.

Following this activity, each person shared some of their dreams with the person sitting next to them. Joylyn happened to be

sitting next to someone who knew her in their community. After the activity he volunteered, *"This is amazing, I never knew that about her."* He was commenting regarding all of Joylyn's dreams that involved helping others in the community—single moms, fatherless children, people with addictions… He had only known her as a victim of society.

When the facilitator asked how this made him feel toward her, he immediately responded, *"She's beautiful."* As you can imagine, the atmosphere was powerful and Joylyn looked more than a little awkward. The facilitator then turned to her and asked her how this made her feel. Her response is one he will never forget: ***"For the first time in my life I feel valuable."***

Four months later, Joylyn was employed full-time at the same Community Center. She is doing case management and helping in all the areas she had dreamed of.

> *The thief does not come except to steal,*
> *and to kill, and to destroy.*
> *I have come that they may have life,*
> *and that they may have it more abundantly.*
>
> John 10:10

are all dreams important?

It is obvious that Martin Luther King, Jr.'s dream was a whole lot bigger than he alone could accomplish. In communicating his dream that day in 1963, it was said of him, *"By speaking the way he did, he educated, he inspired, he informed not just the people there, but people throughout America and unborn generations."* (*A Dream Remembered*, News Hour, 2003.)

That some achieve great success, is proof to all that others can achieve it as well.

~ Abraham Lincoln

So, do all of my dreams have to impact the world? Are my small dreams just as valid? Am I allowed to have dreams that just involve me? Am I insignificant or unimportant if my dreams aren't as big as Martin Luther King, Jr.'s dream?

All your dreams *are* important. Launching *Dream Culture,* the *Dream Coaching Program* at Bethel Church in Redding, California, has been a fun journey. We have seen that God is truly interested in *every* part of people's lives, not just the "spiritual" things or the things that benefit other people. It is also amazing to see how every aspect of someone's life—dreams, experiences, personality, culture—all contribute toward who God made them to be and who they are becoming. Even the things that seem like failures or mistakes can be used for good. Life is a treasure hunt of discovering the gold hidden in us and in others. Every dream and desire is a clue to discovering that treasure!

One of our Dreamers listed a dream to go Big Game Fishing. How significant is that in the scheme of life and death, poverty and injustice, or Heaven and hell? However, just two weeks after our first meeting (we didn't even discuss the dream), the Dreamer was contacted by a church in Miami, Florida where he was scheduled to speak in a couple of months. The church host stated, *"I know you are supposed to leave here on the Monday after the conference, but we were wondering if you would like to delay your return flight because we have the best Big Game Fishing in the world and we would like to take you fishing on that Monday."*

Our Dreamer thought to himself, *"Are you kidding? Does God really love me or is He into Big Game Fishing?"*

Is it possible that the God of all Creation is trying to communicate something to us? He really does love us and delights in us more than we can imagine! Just like a father with his child's birthday wish list, God watches over us and loves to surprise us with His goodness!

> *Life is a treasure hunt, discovering the gold hidden in ourselves and in others.*
>
> *Every dream is a clue toward discovering that hidden treasure.*

Is it possible we're so busy being worried about what He wants us to be, to do or to have, when all along He's saying, *"What do **you** want?"* What father doesn't want the best for his kids? Kris Vallotton, senior associate pastor at Bethel Church, gives a powerful illustration of this in describing a child's interaction with his father one Christmas. Imagine that a child walks up to his father and says to him, *"Dad, this year it's not about me. I just want the perfect thing that's in your heart that you want to give me."* The father is a little surprised at this approach and asks his son, *"Are you serious? What do **you** want?"* The son again seriously states that he only wants what is in his father's heart; what his Dad's perfect will or desire is to give him. The father continues to grow more perplexed, wondering what has come over his son. Finally, after going forwards and backwards in this exercise for a while, the father declares to his son, *"Son, I love you; my heart is only for you. I want to know what you want for Christmas because that is the perfect thing I want to give you."* There is a long pause as this begins to register in the son's imagination. Finally, the son replies, *"Okay, Dad. I'd love a bright red toy fire engine."* The father instantly replies, *"Perfect! Perfect! That is what is in my heart to give you! That is my perfect desire for you this Christmas."*

> *God doesn't see things as spiritual or natural, secular or sacred...*
>
> *to God* EVERYTHING *is natural.*
>
> – Bill Johnson

How is it that religion has so clouded our view of our heavenly Father that we approach Him as orphans or slaves rather than as His own precious, chosen children for whom He has paid the ultimate price? How have we become so conformed to an image of what a believer is *supposed* to look like that we have shut down the very expression of life that each of us carries? Jesus came to demonstrate a Father so in love, so overwhelmingly good, so abundantly generous, that we should all be falling over ourselves to be with Him and with those who represent Him. He came that we might have life, a life overflowing with His unlimited resources. Jesus is coming back for a bride and a friend, not a servant or a slave. So what image of the Father do you communicate to those around you? He made you with desires, with dreams, with passions and He loves to see you come alive, as your dreams become reality. He even hides himself in the journey of your dreams so that all along the journey you discover Him more and more. Just as a father delights over his son catching a ball or his daughter learning to roller blade, so also our Father delights in us.

You see things and say 'Why?'

But I dream things and say, 'Why not?'

- George Bernard Shaw

A Dreamer shared a story of how she had two dreams, one to go to the Olympic games and one to go to Canada. On the surface neither dream appeared to be a *world changing,* significant dream. But both dreams came true when a client offered to pay her way to an Olympic event in Canada. The really fun part about this story is that while she was there, fulfilling her fun dreams, God *interrupted* her and used the event to speak to her specifically about her future. As she walked into the huge arena where the figure skating event was taking place, she felt almost overwhelmed by the sense that *she* would take center stage in this kind of arena in the future. God used her dream of attending the Olympics as part of the way He spoke to her to bring her other dreams to life. You never know how God wants to use your fun dreams to communicate more about your destiny.

Another Dreamer had a *big* dream of speaking in the United States House of Representatives. Aside from that dream, she had a personal dream of being able to sing better—for no other reason than to be able to sing confidently in a crowd and not feel embarrassed.

So in the process of Dream Coaching, she made a goal of taking singing lessons for six months. At the end of six months, her confidence and

Champions aren't made in the gym.

Champions are made from something they have deep inside them - a desire, a dream, a vision.

~ Muhammad Ali

ability had grown significantly and suddenly we all realized that in achieving her *lesser* dream, she had unknowingly prepared and positioned herself for the *big* dream of speaking in the House of Representatives.

There are many different kinds or categories of dreams and *all* are equally important. The Western or Greek mindset tends to compartmentalize different aspects of life and then value each of them differently. But the Eastern (and Hebrew) way of thinking does not separate one part of life from another. Whatever you do is intertwined with all other aspects of *your life* and the lives of people around you. As Bill Johnson, senior pastor of Bethel Church states, *"God doesn't see things as spiritual or natural, secular or sacred... to God everything is natural."*

You never know how God wants to use your fun dreams to communicate more of your destiny.

endless possibilities

So what kinds or types of dreams are there? Below we have listed some different dream categories with a few examples of each. These are certainly not exhaustive, but rather are intended to spark your imagination and broaden your horizons about what dreams can be. There is also a list of Dream Starters in the Dream Resources in the back of this book. The possibilities are endless!

sample dreams

Big Dreams : *End global poverty; find a cure for AIDS; become the first woman president.*

Fun Dreams : *Ride in a hot air balloon; eat a tub of ice cream with friends; ride a unicycle.*

Things to Be : *A great husband and father; physically fit; a source of wisdom to those around me.*

Things to Do : *Graduate from college; climb a mountain; get married.*

Things to Have : *A healthy family; our own home; my own business.*

Spiritual Dreams : *Be known as a friend of God; see creative miracles; live from love.*

Physical Dreams : *Run a marathon; beat an illness; go skydiving.*

Financial Dreams : *Become debt free; give a house to each of my children; give a financial inheritance to my grandchildren.*

Legacy Dreams : *Pay for my grandchildren's education; see my children go further than me in God.*

Emotional Dreams : *Overcome fear; restore a broken relationship; make more friends.*

> *If your dream isn't big enough to scare you,*
>
> *it isn't big enough.*

~ Kenneth Hagin

dream activation exercise

step one | **Starting Your Dream List**

Now it's time to start writing down some of your dreams. We will explore this more in later chapters, but for now we just want to get you started. You will likely want to add to this over the next few days or weeks. The Dream List is your list, so you can add to it or change it at any time. Begin to write down your dreams in whatever order they come to you

Consider the following categories:

— Things to be

— Things to do

— Things to have

Now, for each of the above, consider these different aspects of your life and the lives of those around you:

— Physical

— Financial

— Emotional

— Spiritual

— Legacy

Go back over the sample dream categories at the end of this chapter to trigger more of your dreams. You may also want to go over the Dream Starters in the Dream Resources in the back of this book. There are several different lists to suit different personality types.

DREAM *culture*

why be a dreamer?

It costs nothing to dream;
It costs everything not to.

— Rodney White, *Artist*

So what's the big deal? Why should I even consider being a Dreamer? I've been living safely and comfortably for the last decade, doing what I was told, coloring within the lines, turning up for work on time, serving in my area of ministry and doing what I need to do. Why consider anything more?

We have found that there are some highly convincing reasons for being a Dreamer *and* living your dreams. But more than that, *"God had a dream and wrapped your body around it."* (Lou Engle, www.TheCall.com)

God is the greatest Dreamer of all and it is impossible to encounter Him without being reminded of who we are – children made in His image. One of the greatest things in life is to become increasingly creative by partnering with God's creative nature and

thereby experiencing the joy of His presence. As we live out of that place we see everything around us become fully alive. You always have a choice, but there is no substitute for choosing life! Graveyards throughout the world are full of buried dreams.

So, why be a dreamer?

you have a divine mandate

God made each and every person with the potential to positively affect the world. Gifts, skills, passions and personality combine to uniquely equip you to impact the world around you in a way that no other person can.

You have more than just divine authority to pursue your dreams. You have a divine mandate! Divine authority implies that you can *choose* to pursue your dreams and that, if you do so, Heaven will *back* you. A divine mandate is more compelling. It implies that all of Heaven is pulling on you to pursue your dreams because that is who you were made to be. When you embrace who you were created to become, it is impossible for the people and the planet around you to *not* be impacted in a significant way.

> *Graveyards around the world are full of buried dreams.*

The *cloud of witnesses* mentioned in Hebrews 12:1 is cheering each of us on to live out our dreams and become all that we are called to be. When we embrace who we are and begin to live from a place of purpose, then we can have the greatest impact on the people around us and the Kingdom of Heaven is advanced.

all creation is waiting for you

The Holy Spirit spoke through Paul in his letter to the Christians in Rome that *all creation* groans and waits for the revealing of the sons of God (*see* Romans 8:18-19). The context of this passage is that the glory of God is revealed in us. When Paul is talking about the glory of God being revealed through the sons of God, he is not talking about the glory of God coming down on us as a cloud, but rather that the glory of God would be shown, displayed and revealed *in*

The glory of God is a man fully alive.

~ St. Irenaeus

us. You cannot have the glory of God revealed in you and have people *not* notice! The earth is waiting for us to reveal who God really is by demonstrating His glory, which is His goodness. That revelation comes as each of us encounter God, discover who we are and walk into the fullness of our life in Him.

Our dreams are simply a vehicle for us to tap into who we were designed and fashioned to be. What things are lying dormant in you that God wants to awaken in order to show Himself to the world? Jesus made it possible for us to live our lives in the *fullness* of the glory of God.

life is released all around you

"Hope deferred makes the heart sick, but a desire fulfilled is a **tree of life***"* (*see* Proverbs 13:12). We have all felt the *heart sickness*

of having a dream that hasn't become a reality. However, God wants us to move into a life of walking in the fulfillment of our dreams. When you and I begin to walk in the things that God made for us, life is released all around us. Is it possible that this is a key to divine health?

Recently I was in a meeting where a speaker asked how many people could think of anyone who was doing what they were made to do. Of the hundred or so people in the meeting, only two or three individuals could think of someone who was doing what they were born to do. That is tragic! God's desire for us is that we are *all* doing what we were designed to do, or at the very least, to be intentionally walking toward that.

CREATED TO RUN

Eric Liddell (1902-1945) was an Olympic gold medalist, Scottish international rugby player, and missionary to China. He said of himself, *"God made me fast, and when I run, I feel His pleasure."* His athletic life and Olympic pursuit is depicted in the Oscar-winning 1981 film *Chariots of Fire*.

Eric had a dream to win Olympic gold in his best event, the 100-meter race. Due to Eric's Christian devotion, he refused to run on Sundays. In spite of his dream of a gold medal, when the 1924 Paris Olympics schedule placed the 100-meter race on a

Sunday, Eric withdrew from this event. Instead, a few months before the event, he switched his training to the 400-meter competition since that event was scheduled on a different day of the week. He was not favored to win this event.

When Eric went into the blocks for the start of the 400-meter race, he was handed a slip of paper with a quote from I Samuel 2:30, *"...those who honor Me I will honor..."*

Not only did Eric go on to win gold, but he also broke the existing world record! A few days earlier he had won the Olympic bronze medal for the 200-meter event.

"God made me fast, and when I run, I feel His pleasure."

Source: http://en.wikipedia.org/wiki/Eric_Liddell

It is a beautiful thing to see people doing what they were made for. They come to life. There is a sense of fulfillment and joy, and everyone around them knows it. What would churches look like if every believer pursued his or her dreams rather than trying to be a carbon copy of the pastor or worship leader… where people were encouraged and empowered to fully express themselves? It would be a church that was highly attractive to believer and non-believer alike.

Every person, regardless of race or religion, has the desire to be happy, to be fully alive and to feel significant. What is stopping

you from discovering and pursuing your dream, and in doing so, releasing life, hope and courage to all those around you?

we must dream bigger in order to see global transformation

The earth is our inheritance, and we are Christ's inheritance. Any global problem is *our* problem, because *we* own the planet. So how do we not only solve the problems of the world, but also create an atmosphere on earth that mirrors the splendor of Heaven? We need to transform culture on a global scale. We need every person to embrace who he or she was made to be and contribute what he or she carries. Global Transformation is entirely possible when we each accept that living our God-given dream is the way to affect our community, our city, our nation and every other nation.

What cure to some disease is waiting to be unlocked in the person next door? What song that unites a people group is waiting to be written through the life of your classmate? Perhaps you have a dream to influence government, or science or the arts. Perhaps your dream is to rid the world of AIDS, poverty or injustice. Fantastic! The world needs your dream to become a reality in order to change the realm of society that you are called to influence.

> *Global Transformation is entirely possible when we each accept that living our God-given dream is the key to affect our community, our city, our nation and every other nation.*

Become who you are called to be. Live

it large and let us all bring about Global Transformation that sees the kingdoms of this world become the Kingdom of our God. (*See* Revelation 11:15).

heaven is waiting

God is excited about your dreams. You were His dream from before Creation! As our Creator and Father, He is longing to partner with us and release the resources of Heaven to help us on our way. All of Heaven is waiting! Is it possible that all we need to do is align ourselves with Heaven's values, God's purposes and His design—the way He made us and the things He prepared for us to do—and then we will see a significant release of all the resources we need to make it happen?

In Habakkuk 2:2 we read, *"...Write the vision and make it plain. That he may run who reads it."*

Is it possible that this is not only talking about writing the vision to make it plain for the people on your team, but  *God is excited about your dreams.* also for the angelic *team* that has been assigned to you to help you fulfill your assignment? Angels are waiting to receive their assignments to help us. It is time for us to start partnering with the heavenly host.

We have seen an amazing release of resources as people have written down their dreams and then watched things miraculously fall into place. One man wrote of his dream to learn Spanish. Within two weeks his landlord arrived on his doorstep and offered him an expensive Spanish learning kit that she had ordered and

was unable to return. *"Would you like it?"* she asked the Dreamer.

Another person wrote down a specific dream for a rent-free accommodation. Before she even met with her Dream Coach she was offered a beautiful place to live for only the cost of utilities! One man wrote down that he wanted permanent, rather than occasional, temporary employment. Within 24 hours of writing this down, his employer offered him a permanent position with increased hours.

Time after time we have seen things miraculously come together for Dreamers just a short time after they wrote a Dream List. This does not negate the need for Dreamers to take responsibility and actively pursue their dreams, but writing a Dream List partners with the desire of Heaven to support our endeavors and to actively participate with us.

What is Heaven waiting for you to say *YES* to?

dream activation exercise

This Dream Activation Exercise is designed to highlight the unique expression of who you are and what you bring to the earth. The first three steps below help you in the process of discovering who you are. The fourth step below helps capture some of the ingredients that make you unique.

First we are going to have a look at some of your past successes and how they have something to say about who you are. Ask the Holy Spirit to help, and take your time.

step one | **Remembering**

Think back over your life up to now. Consider the different stages – childhood, adolescence, early adulthood, and so on. Recall your sport, work, family or community experiences.

— For each of these, what was your greatest success or where did you feel most alive?

— Think about, and then list, the ingredients of this event that brought you life. Include such things as individual or team success, your talents or gifts that were in operation, and the platform or place where you thrived.

— Recall the greatest challenges that you have overcome.

— What were some of the other significant

experiences in your life that have helped shape who you are?

step two | **Unpacking The Memories**

Many times we will see something in someone else's life that resonates with something in our own. Maybe that is someone you aspire to be like, or you saw them doing something a certain way that triggered a heart response in you to do something similar. Consider the following questions:

— Thinking back over your list of successes, challenges and significant moments, ask the Holy Spirit to help you identify any themes or ingredients that are repeated.

— For example, perhaps you were involved in the student council in high school and helped build a community center as a young adult. On the surface these have little in common but when you look more deeply it may be that there is a theme of working as a part of a team to achieve something significant. This tells you one aspect of who God made you to be.

There will be many clues to the unique person you are in the many experiences that have made up your life. Do not discount periods of time when you were not walking with the Lord as the gifts and abilities He implanted in you were still in operation during that time.

We have met with many people who have discovered, to their amazement, key events that happened in their lives before encountering Christ. These events also provide clues and insights into who God made them to be. This is especially the case with people who become followers of Christ later in life.

step three | **Who Inspires You?**

Many times we see something in someone else's life that resonates with something in our own. People who inspire you carry a key as to who God made you to be. In order to grasp that key, we need to identify the aspect of their life that inspires us. How this works out could look very different through your life but the ingredients could be similar. Consider the following questions:

— Who inspires you (past or present)?

— Which aspect of their life resonates within you?

— How could that be demonstrated through your life?

step four | **Who Are You?**

You are the only one like you that has ever, or will ever exist. You are unique. You have unique strengths, experiences, capabilities and a personality unlike anyone else. So take some time to connect with your Father in Heaven and ask yourself in His Presence some of the following questions:

— How are you unique?

— What is valuable to you? What is beautiful to you?

— Which situations or circumstances stir you to action or emotion? What are you passionate about?

— If you could change any one thing in the world, what would it be? How could you play a part in that?

Your answers to these questions help highlight the unique expression of who you are and what you bring to the earth.

how do i discover my dreams?

Before I formed you in the womb I knew you;
Before you were born I sanctified you...

Jeremiah 1:5

When we were young, we had no problem dreaming. As children, we fully believed we could be all that was in our hearts to be. Take a brief look into a kindergarten class and you will see countless five-year-olds who are *practicing* their dream to be famous rock stars, ballerinas, presidents, astronauts and superheroes. It never crosses their minds that there are obstacles or barriers to their dreams becoming a reality. However, by the time we grow up, we have been schooled in the ways of the world, and well-meaning adults have *conditioned* us to believe that dreams usually don't come true. We have been taught to bring the size of our dreams down to something that is easily achievable so we won't be disappointed. For many of us, the journey of life has sucked the ability to dream out of us, and left us without a conscious awareness of what is really in our hearts.

awaken your dreams

So how do we reawaken again the desire and ability to dream? There are a number of practical ways to tap into what God has placed in your heart, but first and foremost is to connect with the One who gave us our dreams in the first place. Spend time in the Presence of the Lord and allow Him to reawaken the dormant dreams inside your heart and soul. Ask the Holy Spirit to breathe on your dreams and bring them to life again. Become conscious of His goodness and His ability, rather than focus on all the reasons why your dreams could not come to pass. Refuse to think about the *how* questions; instead, just allow God to embrace you and show you the possibilities. Choose to shrug off any limitations of not enough money, time or resources. For a moment, toss away the inadequacies that you feel, and dream as if you were the absolute best version of yourself, filled with His goodness, His power and His anointing.

DREAMING AFTER RETIREMENT

At age 61, when **Colleen** arrived at Bethel Church, she didn't believe there were any more dreams waiting to be fulfilled in her life. She had built her dream home, raised four children, worked as a national education consultant, was finishing her doctorate degree, and was now retired with too much time on her hands and feeling like life was over. *"I felt old,"* she said.

*"My motto in life for everyone else was, 'Go for your dreams,' but I no longer seemed to have purpose or feel needed. **At this age I had no clue that God still had a plan for my life and so I stopped dreaming.**"*

Colleen realized that she was surrounded by people with similar feelings when she came to the Introduction to Dream Coaching meeting. Soon, the words, encouragement and stories she heard gave her the inspiration she needed to believe she still had gifts from God waiting to be used. She made a list of 100 dreams and suddenly she saw how her doctorate degree in education could lead her into a future, serving God with a greater level of influence than she had ever dreamed possible.

"I decided to go full-out," Colleen remembers, *"and I committed **the rest of my life** to Jesus Christ. It seemed that God had brought me into a Culture of Dreamers..."*

I knew that my life wasn't ending, it was just beginning."

imagine

What would you do and what would you look like if you were fearless? What would you do if you were ten times more courageous? Step away from the realm of the impossible and fly into the realm where *anything is possible for those who believe (see* Mark 9:23). It is in this place that dreams flourish.

Now that you're thinking from a heavenly perspective, begin to look into your heart and discover what's there. Ask yourself what you would do if you had no limitations and no fear of failure. Imagine what the perfect job would be or what the perfect day would be for you. Think on the things you would like to be, to do and to have. Where have you always wanted to go? Who have you always wanted to meet? What would you do if money were not a limitation? *(There are more questions in the Dream Resources section at the back of this book.)* Give yourself permission to have fun and just dream. Nothing is impossible!

Another way to tap into your heart is to remember a time when you felt most alive, and then look at what it was about that experience that made it life giving for you. Maybe you helped with an after-school program and loved it, but now you can't stand the thought of working with children. What was it about that experience that brought you life? Perhaps it was empowering the children to create beautiful paintings. Perhaps it was being part of a team that worked together to accomplish a common goal. If you can uncover why the experience was great for you, you have found another piece of your dream puzzle. Remember that discovering and fulfilling your dreams is a journey, an adventure with God, so relax and enjoy the ride.

> *Our chief want is someone who will inspire us to be what we know we could be.*
>
> ~ Ralph Waldo Emerson

Another way to tap into your dreams is to discover what you are passionate about. What do you stay up late to talk about? What makes you angry? What gets you excited? What do your friends say makes you *come alive?* These are just some of the clues hidden in your heart waiting to be discovered and pursued. Perhaps you feel something stirring when you see social injustice, or you feel strongly moved hearing any story that involves a child in distress. Maybe you could talk for hours about the planets beyond our own galaxy or the billions of organisms hosted on a coral reef. Maybe you are wired for

Remember that discovering and fulfilling your dreams is a journey, an adventure with God, so relax and enjoy the ride.

some little-known sport or lie awake every night thinking about playing in a Super Bowl. Whatever your passion may be, take the time to listen as God reveals to you what He is awakening within you. Who knows whether you will be the next Joan of Arc, Benjamin Franklin, Martin Luther King, Jr. or Mother Teresa?

The last thing we want to say about starting the Dream Journey is to realize that it *is* a journey and that we are all at different places on this journey. Where you are now is fine, but continue to intentionally move forward in your dreams. So many people are anxious about not knowing the *big dream* for their lives. They compare themselves with other people who seem to have their dreams all figured out and they feel bad that they're not there yet.

It's hard to dream when you feel bad about yourself and put yourself under pressure to come up with an answer. Instead, take the pressure off yourself and enjoy the journey of discovery. God has made you unique, and He wants to go with you on

a journey of discovery. This journey is to find what's in your heart. Every dream, no matter how small, is a part of who God made you to be and is a valuable piece of the treasure hunt. So give yourself permission to be wherever you are on the road and enjoy the journey!

PERMISSION TO DREAM

During one Dream Coaching session, I had a remarkable experience. We had been talking for about an hour when the Dreamer took a sip of coffee and then suddenly turned red in the face. Tears squirted from her eyes. The reaction was so dramatic I thought she had scalded her throat on hot coffee. I offered her a sip of my ice water to soothe her throat then realized that her coffee had been sitting for an hour; it was no longer hot enough to scald anyone! What had happened that had caused such a dramatic reaction?

As she composed herself, I quickly tried to think back to grasp what I might have said to upset her. In a few moments she recovered and was able to explain that she had seen **a hand from Heaven come down and stamp her dream with the word "APPROVED." For the first time ever, she felt permission to dream.**

This encounter with the Father gave her courage to pursue her dream of manufacturing a product that would eventually be made by women coming out of prostitution, giving them financial security. At the time of writing this book, she is working with a company to produce the prototype of that product.

 dream activation exercise

step one | **Permission to Dream**

Take some time to direct your thoughts toward Heaven and experience His Presence with you. Meditate on who He is.

Meditate on Mark 1:11 and Luke 15:31:

> "You are my beloved son/daughter, in whom I am well pleased."
>
> "Son/Daughter, you are always with Me and all I have is yours."

Consider who you are in Him. Let go of the obstacles, restraints and limitations that you are acutely aware of because of past experiences. After a time of just enjoying Him, start to make the following declarations over your life. Pause after each, and repeat them until they become a reality for you:

> I am a child of God.
>
> His Presence surrounds me.
>
> I have permission to dream.
>
> I have permission to be me.
>
> I have permission to try new things.
>
> I have permission to fail.

I have permission to learn from my experiences.

I have permission to create.

I have permission to succeed.

Nothing is impossible.

step two | **100 Dreams Exercise**

Go back to the Dream List that you started from the Dream Activity at the end of chapter two. Now it's time to write out more of your dreams. We suggest going for 100 dreams because that will challenge you to go beyond the surface and explore more of what is in your heart.

Find a place and time that works for you. That may be with a coffee in your hand sitting in a Starbucks, or alone in the woods surrounded by nature. How do you connect best with your Father and tap into your capacity to dream?

If it is helpful look over the Dream Starters listed in the Dream Resources at the back of this book. And remember:

Nothing is impossible!

step three | **Dream Cache**

A Dream Cache is the place you record your dreams so you can return to them in the future. Your Dream Cache should be something that is at your fingertips when you want it and inspires you when you look at it. It should also allow you to record when you've reached a dream. It's tremendously encouraging to look back and see all the dreams you've fulfilled!

Your Dream Cache doesn't have to be just a list on your computer. Look over the following options (or make up one of your own) and choose one that fits you and you would love to use.

Dream Board — Take a bulletin board and put up lists, pictures, sketches and other articles that represent your dreams. If you are a visual person, seeing your dreams will inspire you whenever you look at them.

Dream Journal — Use a battered old notebook or a special leather-bound journal with hand-made paper pages. What kind of book would you like to use to record your dreams? You may choose to make this a place to not only record your dreams but also to record the journey that you are on, and the thoughts, fears and successes you have along the way.

Your Computer — Make a simple list of your dreams or add pictures from the Internet to create a sideshow or screensaver to display your dreams. Do what works best for you. Make it inspiring and give yourself a reason to look at it over and over.

Dream Poster — Write your dreams on a sheet of poster board and put it on the wall or find a poster that inspires you and write your dreams on it. You might even take one of your big dreams, find a picture of it, frame it, and hang it on your office wall.

Dream Box — Find one item that represents each one of your dreams and treasure it in a special box. You may even find other items, words or articles that you can display on a bookshelf or another conspicuous place to remind you of your dreams.

step four | **Record Your Dreams**

Transfer the dreams you've jotted down so far into your Dream Cache. Continue to increase your Dream List, adding to it or altering it as you are inspired.

beliefs to build a dream on

...and the rain descended, the floods came,
and the winds blew and beat on the house; and it did not
fall, for it was founded on the rock.

Matthew 7:25

It's one thing to dream or have a dream. It's another thing to turn that dream into reality. Turning your dream from an idea into reality takes a lot of courage as well as intentionally making daily choices that create forward momentum.

In the construction industry, one of the first steps in turning a building plan into an actual building is to establish a solid foundation. Without a solid foundation, the first storm will send the building crashing to the ground. In order to establish a life of living your dreams, it is important to first check your foundation. What are the beliefs or core values that are necessary to live a life of dreams being fulfilled?

We believe the following foundational beliefs are necessary in order to build a life of consistently fulfilling dreams. We have

turned these beliefs into core values that we must live out—where other people also see these things happening in our lives. We encourage you to examine your own beliefs and invite the Holy Spirit to lead you into a place of encountering more of Him so that, in turn, more of Heaven can be experienced around you.

God is good all the time

Our foundational core value is: God is good, period. His goodness is continually expressed to us. Take a moment to think on that truth. Right now, how is God's goodness being expressed to you personally? When was the last time you stopped to even think about how good He is to you? Take a few minutes to really stop and think about how He is pouring out His goodness to you in this current season of your life. How aware are you of God's goodness, especially as it pertains to you?

At the time of writing this part of the book, it's fall in Redding, and the colors are particularly glorious. Each day as I drive our children to school, and see the early morning light filter through the trees, I am grateful to the Lord for this expression of His nature. My children are getting used to hearing me say, *"The color of the trees right now just makes me happy."* I choose to focus on the goodness of the Lord expressed to me in this season through nature. I experience a childlike delight in the different colors of the leaves and in the crispness of the air as I walk in the mornings. I choose to believe that the brilliant, red sunrises and sunsets are painted just for me by a Daddy who knows that I love bright colors. And, in a way, they are painted just for me, because I know He loves me enough to paint them just for my eyes, even if I were the only one there to see them.

The world around us speaks of God's extravagance. There are myriads of flowers and plants created that process carbon dioxide or provide food for animals, yet that function is secondary to the beauty they bring to the planet. I am amazed at the diversity of God's creation, and convinced that He did it with us in mind, just for us to enjoy the beauty of the colorful flowers. And it's extravagant. Not wasteful, but extravagant. It reminds me that His heart is always to bless me, to

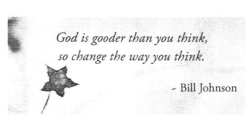

God is gooder than you think, so change the way you think.

- Bill Johnson

give me more than just what is needed, to give abundantly. It demonstrates a part of His nature that infiltrates every part of who He is — that He is good. Not just a little bit good, but extravagantly good!

*"How great is the love the Father has **lavished** on us, that we should be called children of God! And that is what we are!"* (*See* I John 3:1, *emphasis added*). He has *lavished* His love on us. The *Collins English Dictionary* defines lavish as, *"prolific, abundant, generous, liberal and extravagant."* And the verse above says that this is the measure with which God pours out His love on us. He doesn't give us just enough of His love to survive; He pours out with the most abundant measure He can find. Jesus did not just provide a way into Heaven, but He made a way for us to enter into a life overflowing with His abundance, *now*.

He is a loving Father, full of goodness and mercy. He is pouring out His love on you. Are you receiving it? You may not have had a natural father that showed you what this love looks like. But even a great earthly father can only give you a taste of your heavenly Father's goodness; and God wants to show His goodness to you.

After we had been married a few years, Andy's parents moved to a different city a few hours drive away from where we lived. Sometimes we would drive over to stay the weekend with them. I can remember being embarrassed by the way that Andy, immediately upon arrival, would go to the refrigerator and help himself to the chocolate cookies that would be there. I felt that it was rude for Andy to help himself to whatever was in the pantry or refrigerator because he no longer lived with his parents. Andy's mom however, loved it. She loved that he felt comfortable enough with his place in the family to get what he desired. I realized after a few visits that she usually only had chocolate cookies in the house when we were there and that they had been placed there especially for Andy.

God has a refrigerator full of good things for you and me, just ready for us to help ourselves. He has physical and emotional healing for us. He has provision for us and He has love and encouragement waiting there specifically for us. The cupboards of Heaven are fully stocked with an abundance of His goodness just for us. The question is: Will you come and raid His pantry?

Psalm 34:8 says, *"Oh taste and see that the Lord is good…"* This is an invitation for us to respond. When someone offers you a taste of a freshly baked cookie just out of the oven, the natural response is to reach out, take the cookie and take a bite. It's obvious there needs to be action on your part to receive or experience the goodness of the cookie that has been offered to you. If you don't reach out and take one, put it to your lips, and take a bite, you can only imagine how those cookies taste. There is no difference in experiencing the goodness of God. You must, figuratively speaking, reach out your hand, take what is offered and taste His goodness. Whether or not you do that is largely determined by what you believe about your Father. If you believe your Father is not good, or is not good to you, then you will think that the cookies He offers you will taste bad or are even poisoned. You will be reluctant to partake of His goodness in case it doesn't turn out to be good at all. But, if you are truly aware of His goodness, you will readily respond to His invitation and reach out to receive what He has for you. In fact, once you experience His goodness, you will look for it everywhere and you will find it. You will readily accept the offer of more "cookies" from your Father's hand as you discover just how good He is.

We live in a fallen world and there are challenges to face every day that come with living in this world. Whether or not I see the goodness of God in my surroundings will be determined by what I choose to set my eyes on. If I set my eyes to look for negative things, I will easily find them, and I can convince myself that God doesn't care. But if I set my eyes to see how He's pouring out His goodness to me today, I will find it in abundance. There is not a day that goes by that there is not something for which we can be grateful. My Daddy is a good Father who lavishes His love upon me. His love is always directed at me, no matter

where I am, what I'm doing, or who I'm with. He is totally for me and wants to pour out blessing on me.

> *God be merciful to us and bless us,*
> *and cause His face to shine upon us,*
> *that Your way may be known on earth,*
> *Your salvation among all nations.*

Psalm 67:1-2

> *I will make you a great nation;*
> *I will bless you and make your name great;*
> *and you shall be a blessing.*

Genesis 12:2

These verses talk about God's desire to bless us because He loves us and because He loves those who don't yet know Him. His desire is that other people would look at our lives and see the goodness of God so evidenced that they would be drawn to know the God we know. It is by experiencing His kindness and goodness that we are lead to repentance. Our lives are intended to be evidence to the world that God is good.

We have four children, and like most children, they love sweet treats. And I love to bless them. I love to give them good things and see their faces light up when they get an unexpected gift. However, my role as a parent requires more than just giving them treats. I have the responsibility to do what I can to teach them how to live a healthy lifestyle.

So, although I love to bless them, the fact is they must eat a well balanced diet to have strong bodies, and too much candy is not good for their teeth. To my children, I'm sure there are times when they feel I am withholding good things from them (like the candy they know is hidden in the cupboard). But, as they have grown older and we have taught them about healthy lifestyles, they have come to appreciate that withholding candy is my gift to them, in order to protect their health. They know that if I am saying *NO* to treats, I am saying *YES* to health. They have learned that my denying them candy comes from a great love for them and a heart for them to have the best.

> *Our lives are intended to be evidence to the world that God is good.*

Psalm 84:11 declares that the Lord *withholds* no good thing. Our heavenly Father knows what needs to be included for our greater good. He knows what our bodies, souls and spirits need in order to thrive. He loves to lavish good gifts on us, but like any wise father, He knows when to hold back in order to give us the greater gift.

God is love, so anything that is not found in love is not of God. Sickness, disease, pain, brokenness, war and all other evil things do not have their origins in God. When Jesus died on the cross for us, He took all the wrath of God for our past, present and future sin. The result is that through Christ, we can continually experience the goodness of God. The sufferings, hardships and challenges we face in a world that is groaning for the fullness of the restoration of all things, can be transformed within us into good (*see* Romans 8:28)! We may make mistakes and other people may make mistakes that affect us, but God is always good.

> *The goodness of God endures continually.*
>
> Psalm 52:1a

He longs to bless you today and pour His love out on you with a lavish measure. Will you reach out to taste and see that the Lord is good?

A DREAM TO HEAR GOD'S VOICE

Charlie (in his late 20's) had been a Christian all his life but **had never heard God's voice.** This changed following an experience triggered by a Dreaming Presentation in a business where he worked. As a result, he went home and he and his wife each made a list of 100 dreams.

To Charlie's surprise, his wife's number one dream was to have a baby as soon as possible! He thought they had agreed to wait six months before getting pregnant. After going back and forth they decided to pray about it. Charlie's prayer went like this: *"Well God, this is a dream of my wife's, but I think we should wait, so if I need to change my mind about it - You need to tell me loud and clear."* Two days later, one of Charlie's co-workers walked up to him and told him he just had a vision of Charlie and his wife having the exact same conversation and that the Lord had said, *"Be fruitful and multiply."*

This completely altered Charlie's paradigm about how God speaks to us today and launched him on a journey of learning to hear God speak to him. Now God is even giving him information about business deals, and when people will call. He even was given a phone number that turned out to be the number of a school with which he wanted to do business!

As Charlie said: *"Now we are six months pregnant and I've been on a passionate pursuit of God's voice ever since. Dreams are important!"*

---

i have a purpose

We are significant because we are the children of God. As such, we have tremendous value, completely independent of what we do or don't do. We are of great importance because we are children of the King. We are adopted into God's Royal Family and have been given access to His Presence and all the treasure He has for us.

Healing, wholeness, blessing and peace are all available to us because our Daddy loves us. But the story doesn't end there. He didn't create us so we could just sit around in His Presence. He created us with purpose in mind. Right from the beginning, He gave us the task of being fruitful and multiplying, of filling the earth and subduing it (*see* Genesis 1:28). God placed Adam in a garden, and told him to fill the earth. Adam's identity as a son of God was clear. Every day He walked and talked face to face with God in the garden. He worked *from* relationship, from identity, from significance and not in order to obtain relationship, identity or significance. He worked *from* rest, not for rest. In the same way we have identity, significance and intimate relationship with God *and* we have a unique purpose on the earth to fulfill.

God spoke of Jeremiah, saying, *"Before I formed you in the womb*

I knew you; before you were born I sanctified you; I ordained you a prophet to the nations" (Jeremiah 1:5). God had a plan for Jeremiah from before he was in the womb, and He put him together with that purpose in mind. Everything that Jeremiah would need to fulfill the plan God had for him, God placed inside of him as He put him together in his mother's womb. When God commissioned Jeremiah for his purpose, Jeremiah argued with God that he could not speak because he was only a youth (*see* Jeremiah 1:6). However, God remained unimpressed with the protest, knowing that what He had placed inside of Jeremiah was more than sufficient to accomplish all that He had for him to do.

Psalm 139:13-16 declares that God also created *you* as you were being formed in your mother's womb. He wrote all of your days in a book. He took as much care weaving your body, your gifts, your personality and every other part of you together as He did in knitting Jeremiah together. Why? It is because, just like Jeremiah, He wants to establish you as a gift to the world. Jeremiah's purpose was to speak on God's behalf to the nations. God had given Jeremiah what he needed to live out this purpose. You might not be a prophet to the nations, but you have a unique purpose; clues to that purpose are found in your dreams. God uniquely put you together, giving you all you need to become the person He wrote about in His book before you were born. The question is: ***Will you choose to believe you are who He says you are?*** When you live from the reality of being made with a purpose, you will not be satisfied with living a mediocre life. You will be drawn to discover the person God made you to become and the life He made you to lead.

Ephesians 2:10 says, *"…we are His workmanship, created in Christ Jesus for good works, which God prepared beforehand that we should walk in them."* Each one of us is God's workmanship, designed and put together by the Master Craftsman for a unique purpose. Each one of us is specifically designed to be a vital part of the Body, so that together, we can, *"…grow up in all things into Him who is the head – Christ – from whom the whole body, joined and knit together by what every joint supplies, according to the effective working by which **every part does its share,** causes growth of the body…"* (Ephesians 4:15-16, *emphasis added*).

The Body needs you to be fully you in order to function at its best.

The Body needs you to be fully you in order to function at its best. I Corinthians 12 talks extensively about this concept. It details how each part is essential for the whole body to function as it was designed. If you have ever had a sore throat, you know that having even a small part of you in pain can unsettle the whole body. Each of us has been designed to play a vital role in the transformation of planet earth. Each of us has a part to play in displaying who God is through our expression of Him. Whether you are called to be an ear or an eye or something less visible, you are important in the Body. We need you to be fully you, functioning as you were made to function. The cells that make up an eye, and those that make up an ear are very different. A cell made to see is going to have a hard time hearing and will never be as effective as an ear cell in performing that function. Eye cells will perform at their best where they have been designed to function, in the eye.

In the natural world, we understand this concept easily. We all value our heart as an essential part of our bodies, despite not seeing it at work. We do not devalue it because it's invisible. But neither do we try to convert other parts of our body to become the heart. We recognize that each part of our physical body plays a role in our overall well-being. However, when it comes to being part of the Body of Christ, we often devalue ourselves because we don't see how or where our part contributes to the whole of the Body. Yet, whether visible or unseen, each of us carries a vital part of who God is, representing Him and His Kingdom in the earth. Our unique contribution is released as we live out our dreams, as we live out who He designed and purposed us to be. You are significant! You have purpose!

nothing is impossible

God has given us a dream and He is waiting to help us live that dream and positively affect the planet as we do. The problem is that many of us have experienced failure and disappointment in our quest to fulfill our dreams and the process has left us with our

Each of us has been designed to play a vital role in the transformation of planet Earth.

faith in tatters. We start to wonder, *"Is this dream really possible? Can I do what it takes to make this happen?"* Although we mentally agree with the Scripture that nothing is impossible with God, we are not sure that it's true within the context of our own lives (*see* Matthew 19:26).

Truly believing that nothing is impossible is vital to seeing your dreams fulfilled. There is no dream that has the potential to affect the lives of people that will not encounter some level of resistance along the way. It will not always be easy to pursue the dream. Having a strong sense that there is always a way through will keep you going, no matter what your eyes may tell you.

I remember a scene from one of the *Indiana Jones* movies where Indy had instructions to go through a tunnel hewn through rock in search of a certain relic. He knew he was on the right path, but he came to a point where the path suddenly ended. In front of him was an impossible gap between two cliff-like faces, with a deathly, sheer drop between them. He could see the goal on the other side, but there was no way to cross. Being Indiana Jones he looked for something he could use to swing across the gap, but his usual stunts were rendered useless. He was unable to move forward, but if he didn't move forward and get the relic, someone would die.

This is such a great picture of our life of faith. We all have had those moments when it feels like there is no possible way forward; yet, if you don't move forward, your dream will die. In some cases, the dream itself seems impossible from the start. *Before* you get to this point, decide that you are going to take God at His word and believe *there is always a way forward.* It may not look like you expect, and at times you may have to change your approach or take another path, but *there is always a way forward.*

If you don't decide ahead of time that God is the God of the impossible, when you get to a dead-end, you're going to just

throw up your hands in despair and give up. But if you have already determined that nothing is impossible, you will continue to look for the way God has already made available to you to move forward. You will seek and search for what is possible rather than focusing on what is not. In the *Indiana Jones* movie, the hidden way forward was an invisible path across the chasm. When Indy took a step of faith and adjusted the way he was looking (changed his perspective), he was able to see that the path was there all along. He had to first take a step of faith to discover the way before he could advance to win the day.

I was once involved in setting up a new preschool. This was a dream come true, having been unexpectedly approached by another non-profit organization that practically gave us the business and facilities for the balance of their mortgage. We had the building, but it had been poorly maintained and needed to be fully renovated inside and out in order to qualify for government registration and funding.

> *Start by doing what's necessary;*
> *then do what's possible;*
> *and suddenly you are doing*
> *the impossible.*
>
> ~ Saint Francis of Assisi

The timing of this massive undertaking made the task look impossible, so much so that the government official who had to sign off on the license told us we would never do it in time. But God says nothing is impossible. We took God at His word and began to look at what we needed to do, and could do, to make the impossible happen. It wasn't easy. There were plenty of tears, long hours and hard work. But the underlying belief that nothing is impossible kept us looking for the way through that we knew must be there.

I was forever changed in my understanding that nothing is impossible as I saw problem after problem dissolve before us as we partnered with the God of the impossible. When I turned up with the final documentation required for licensing, the surprised government official said, *"I was just telling my colleague that you would never do it in time."* The preschool opened on time and is now a thriving business and an environment where children are taught the ways of God.

In your Dream Journey, there are likely to be many *impossible* situations that try to stop you from reaching your goal. How you respond to these challenges will determine if you hit the target or not. And how you respond will be determined by what you truly believe. Is your God the God of the impossible? Will He come through for you when you are partnering with Him to fulfill the dream He placed inside of you? What does your life say you believe to be true of Him?

NOTHING IS IMPOSSIBLE

Ixil grew up in the coffee-growing mountains of Nicaragua. Life was not promising to the majority of those in her community. Ixil's dream was to get a Master's Degree in Business (MBA) and then use these skills to reduce poverty in her home nation.

Ixil did most of her undergraduate degree through night classes so she could work full-time during the day. Then, through her father's coffee business, she met a man who offered her a scholarship to learn English in England. During one trip home, she "just happened" to meet the prince of a small European country. The prince asked her what her dreams were and she said that she wanted to earn an MBA, but she couldn't afford the tuition. Three months later, the prince initiated another meeting. He told her to find the university she wanted to go to, and that he would cover all of the expenses of her MBA program. The prince covered more than $80,000 of tuition, travel and living expenses, including an allowance!

Ixil is now working on setting up systems for a microfinance institute in Nicaragua. As Ixil says, ***"The circumstances of your life should never determine what your future should look like. If God gives you a dream, it is because He has already backed it up with the provision to go for it."***

i am responsible for me

> *You can lead a horse to water,*
> *but you can't make it drink.*

Old English Proverb

Ultimately, you are the only one responsible for what you do with your life. Your parents, teachers, leaders, friends and enemies are not responsible for the choices you make. You are responsible for you. We will each bring an account to God of what we did with what we had. No one else can do for you what you are designed to do for yourself. No one else can achieve your dreams for you. It starts with ownership. You only have power over what you have taken ownership or responsibility for.

In Matthew 25, Jesus tells a number of stories to illustrate the Kingdom of Heaven. He contrasts ten wise and ten foolish virgins who are waiting for a bridegroom. The wise virgins have taken ownership and responsibility for keeping their lamps stocked with sufficient oil, even though the bridegroom is delayed in coming. The foolish virgins have made no provision and want the wise virgins to provide for their lack. The answer they receive would shock some well-meaning believers: *"... 'No, lest there should not be enough for us and you; but go rather to those who sell, and **buy for yourselves.** '"* (Matthew 25:9, *emphasis added*).

Jesus continues to tell another story illustrating the Kingdom of Heaven. In this story a man goes to a far country, but leaves his servants with different measures of his goods, according to their ability. Each servant receives an amount of talents that he has

the ability to increase through his efforts. One servant receives five talents, another two, and another, one. The first two servants double what they were given and receive the same reward: *"Well done, good and faithful servant; you were faithful over a few things, I will make you ruler over many things. Enter into the joy of your lord,"* (Matthew 25:21, 23). However the third servant buried his talent in the ground because he held a wrong belief concerning his master. He did not take personal responsibility for what he had, but tried to preserve it and protect himself. Many of us do the same thing trying to protect and preserve ourselves because we hold a distorted view of ourselves and of God. We even try to deflect responsibility by saying we buried our talent in good soil.

In the story, the result was disastrous for this servant. He was called wicked and lazy and what he did have was taken from him and given to the servant who had demonstrated ownership and responsibility. (*See* Matthew 25:24 – 30).

I grew up with a personal aversion to self-promotion and anything that looked political. Those around me recognized my leadership gifting (talent), but I was trying to bury it because of a lie or distorted belief I held. This overreaction resulted in me actually avoiding some leadership roles or positions of influence in my workplace for fear of being seen as promoting myself. One day, this pattern came up in a conversation with my pastor and he saw straight through the lie I believed and the resultant burying of my talents. He challenged me with a conversation out of the movie, *Crimson Tide* (1995). Paraphrased, the captain said to an officer, *"There are two kinds of people in the world—those who promote themselves, and those who protect themselves—what kind are you?"* I suddenly had the revelation that I had been preserving myself and, as a result, I was at risk of losing life (*see* Matthew 16:25). I immediately went to my boss acknowledging what had just happened and apologized for avoiding responsibility. I then offered to take on any responsibility that he would like to give me. He was amazed at the turn-around and took me up on the

> *You are not only responsible for what you say, but also for what you do not say.*
>
> ~ Martin Luther

offer. Not only that, but within three months I was promoted to a regional management role! What would have happened, or not happened, if I had continued to avoid responsibility for the talents in my life?

Ownership and responsibility release power to work through decisions and see the opportunities we have in front of us. By avoiding or passing responsibility for our lives (talents, dreams, decisions) to others, we give them our power and embrace powerlessness. Powerlessness is a lie. You are a powerful decision-making being, designed to co-create with God. It's time to take responsibility back and release the power to act from within you. All of Heaven backs you up, but will you back you up?

On the journey to realizing our dreams, we must take responsibility, which is demonstrated by actually doing something. The coaching section of this book will give you practical steps on how to move toward your dreams, but here again it is important to address the question of who is responsible for you. There may be aspects of your dream that are dependent on other people, but keep the focus on what you can do. What is in your hand to accomplish? What are you doing to steward the

*All of Heaven backs you up, but will **you** back you up?*

favor, resources and gifts you have been given? Taking responsibility for your life and stewarding those things well will qualify you for increase. Feeling sorry for yourself and looking at what you can't change will leave you feeling powerless and give you an excuse to do nothing. Focus on what you do have, what you can do. When you focus on what you don't yet have or what is beyond your control to do at the moment, you give away your power and embrace powerlessness. That is not what you were created to be and do.

One way to help you stay responsible, powerful and on track moving toward a dream, is to make yourself accountable to someone you trust. Accountability alone can be a powerful motivator. No one can make you accountable to do something with your life, but you can choose to make yourself accountable to someone. The heart or intention is that the person you make yourself accountable to regularly asks you courageous questions that remind you of your commitment to greatness—to who you really are.

An amusing experience with the power of accountability was illustrated through one of our Dreamers whose action steps included completing two exercise DVD's by her following session. The next session came around and she was asked how she had gotten on with her action steps. She cheerfully filled the coach in on what she had done until she came to the action step involving the DVD exercise classes. At that point, she hung her head in an embarrassed way and starting laughing. When pushed for details, she admitted that she had indeed done the two classes, but that she had done them both the day before, one after the other, much to the amusement of her family.

Her Dream Coach jokingly asked if this program was so scary that she felt she needed to do something like that, rather than just confess that she didn't follow through. *"No,"* she replied, *"It's just that I had made a commitment to myself, I wanted to follow through on it and I knew you would ask me about it."* It's probably a lesson she won't forget in a hurry. Accountability holds us to who we really are. It helps us measure up to our expectations of ourselves, rather than someone else's expectation of us. It demonstrates responsibility and ownership.

In deciding which action steps to proceed with (there may be many) it is important to ensure that you, the Dreamer, have the final say. You are the one responsible for your life and the one that needs the motivation to continue with the changes or actions necessary to pursue your dreams. Don't let anyone tell you what you should do or tell you what works for them. You are a powerful person and God has given you everything pertaining to life and godliness (*see* II Peter 1:3). You are responsible for what you do with your life, and God has already given you what you need to live it successfully.

greatness comes through serving

Let this mind be in you which was also in Christ Jesus,
who, being in the form of God, did not consider it robbery
to be equal with God, but made Himself of no reputation,
taking the form of a bondservant, and coming in the likeness of men.
And being found in appearance as a man, He humbled Himself
and became obedient to the point of death,
even the death of the cross.

Philippians 2:5-8

The final core value we want to mention in the context of this book is the core value of serving. It would be easy to read this book and get the impression that you should just go for your dreams and ignore the needs of others around you. Some have used the

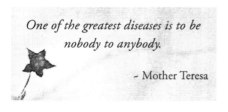

One of the greatest diseases is to be nobody to anybody.

~ Mother Teresa

cry, *"I am not called to this,"* as an excuse to be lazy or irresponsible and not serve the community of which they are a part. Discovering your dreams and pursuing who you are called to be, should not be used to abandon your responsibilities. The fear of many leaders when they hear that people are going after their dreams is that they will become selfish and so focused on going where they are going, that they will lose the value of serving. This should not be the case. Our example is Jesus.

Jesus knew who He was; He knew where He had come from and where He was going (*see* John 8:14). He knew He was God and yet He served those around Him, not as a mindless slave only doing what He was told, but as a Son who partnered with His Father.

As we learn and grow, we become more aware of the gifts and abilities that God has placed within us, and we learn how to use them as a gift to those around us. Those gifts and abilities, in the context of our personal character and maturity, are vehicles we can use to effectively advance the Kingdom of God. That being said, we never graduate to a place where we are above serving in a simple capacity. Our plea to you is that you recognize where you are on the Dream Journey, and that you continue to serve those around you with excellence.

> *But Jesus called them to Himself and said,*
> *"You know that the rulers of the Gentiles lord it over them,*
> *and those who are great exercise authority over them.*
> *Yet it shall not be so among you; but whoever desires to*
> *become great among you, let him be your servant.*
> *And whoever desires to be first among you,*
> *let him be your slave – just as the Son of Man*
> *did not come to be served, but to serve,*
> *and to give His life a ransom for many."*
>
> Matthew 20:25-28

Jesus was, and is, the Ruler of the universe. He is fully God, yet when He came to earth in bodily form, He did not think it beneath Him to serve people. We find Him washing the feet of the disciples at the Last Supper, revealing a beautiful picture of His heart to serve people. He had every right to have someone wait on Him day and night. Yet what we see in the Gospels is a very different picture of Jesus. We find Him serving all, from a begging leper to the governor of Israel. Even when Jesus tried

to get away with His disciples to a deserted place to rest, the multitude figured out where He was headed and were there waiting for Him. When Jesus saw them, He didn't react angrily out of His own need or desire, but instead He was moved with compassion and began to teach them (*see* Mark 6:31-34). Time after time, Jesus demonstrated that He came to serve, not to be served. His greatness was revealed through serving.

What motivated Jesus to do this? What allowed Him to serve people, knowing that He was God and therefore deserving of being served? I believe the answer lies in His love for people and for the Father. Jesus' heart was often moved by compassion, and as His heart was moved, He reached out again and again to heal, express tangible love or teach his followers.

Jesus knew what it was to have His priorities set by Heaven.

But He also saw what the Father was doing and knew how to partner with that. Jesus said that He did nothing of Himself, but only did what He saw His Father doing (*see* John 5:19). Jesus knew what it was to have His priorities set by Heaven. He had a strong sense of accomplishing what the Father had set before Him and becoming who He was; yet He saw clearly that the way to do that was to serve.

We too are on a journey of becoming who He has called us to be. As we chase our dreams, we are really advancing from glory to glory as we become more like Him and more of who He made us to be. That path always includes service. Service is a core value of the Kingdom, and it is one that should not be set aside as we consider chasing our dreams.

There will be seasons, especially when you are younger, or younger in your walk with the Lord, when you serve others outside of your gifting, purpose or personal preference. In many cases, you will find that you discover your purpose in serving. I spent many hours as a young adult serving my local church by copying recorded messages during conferences. I wasn't passionate about this task, or even motivated about people having the opportunity to listen to valuable lessons over and over. I simply chose to align myself with the value of service. The outcome was that I got passionate about serving in a very non-glamorous job that no one knew about. And as I was faithful to serve where I was needed, I grew in my ability to serve the Lord in other areas.

> *You are My friends if you do whatever I command you.*
> *No longer do I call you servants,*
> *for a servant does not know what his master is doing;*
> *but I have called you friends,*
> *for all things that I heard from My Father*
> *I have made known to you.*

John 15:14-15

We begin as a servant, but the invitation is to become His friend. We graduate into knowing what He is doing, working alongside him and co-laboring with Him. Notice that in the passage above, the prerequisite for going from a servant to a friend is first learning to obey (serve), and through serving, you learn what the Master is doing and what's on His heart.

Galatians 3:29 - 4:7 also talks about this process. At the moment we are born again we become heirs of God, but we continue

to live as if we were slaves. As we mature, we move into the place where we are able to operate as sons. Mature sons can be trusted to take care of the family business because they have proven themselves to have the heart of the Father and will carry themselves in a way that accurately represents His heart. This is a life-long process for each of us, but no matter where you are on this journey moving toward an ever increasing intimacy with God, you have a significant role to play on the earth. As you mature into the fullness of who God made you to be, you have an increasing ability to release His presence on the earth through serving people.

God intended the gifts and abilities He placed in you to be offered as a gift to those around you. Genesis 12:2-3 says we are blessed to be a blessing. As you pursue your dreams, never lose sight of the fact that becoming who you are called to be is an opportunity to serve people in a greater and greater way.

Wherever you are on your journey, serve generously and with excellence. Commit yourself to always do your best and to thrive in the environment where you are planted. Choose to have an eye to see what needs to be done and just get busy and do it. Never think you have outgrown simply serving other people. Continue to worship and serve the Lord through serving His people, even when you are the leader in a particular environment. Remember the example of Jesus, and show the Father's love by serving those around you.

dream activation exercise

step one | **Identifying Core Beliefs**

As you read through this section, what thoughts, feelings or revelations did you notice or become aware of about yourself? What do those feelings tell you about what you believe?

It is impossible to truly believe something and not have it evidenced in your life. For example, if you believe that God is good all the time, but expect or accept negative events in your life, then it is likely that your belief is in your mind but not established in your heart. Likewise, if you truly believe nothing is impossible, there will be evidence in your conversation and actions that demonstrate this belief. So, when did you last make conscious steps toward doing the impossible? Do any of your dreams rely on an impossible component?

Now consider the following in regard to identifying your core beliefs:

— How does your life display what you say you believe?

— What would your friends, family or colleagues say your beliefs are judging from the way that they experience you?

— What does your conversation say about what you believe about God and yourself? Remember your audible dialogue reflects your internal thoughts.

— You may consider doing this activity with a friend and

getting some honest feedback about how the way you speak reflects your beliefs

step two | **Changing Core Beliefs**

With God, nothing is impossible! The first step to changing core beliefs is to become aware of truth. God is the Spirit of Truth so the obvious place to access truth is to encounter Him. Transformation starts with a renewal of the mind (repentance means to return to the right thinking).

Take some time to turn your thoughts and attention toward Heaven. Invite the Holy Spirit to give you a Spirit of Wisdom and Revelation in the knowledge of Him. Ask Him to reveal to you and lead you in all Truth. Now take some time and meditate on each of these core beliefs:

— God is good all the time

— I have a purpose

— Nothing is impossible

— I am responsible for me

— Greatness comes through serving

Ask yourself the following questions in regard to each of these core beliefs:

— What would the evidence of these core beliefs look like in your life at this time?

— How would it feel to truly believe each of the above

truths? For example, if you believe you have a purpose, you will feel significant regardless of what is happening in your circumstances.

— Continue to meditate on each truth.
Remember that a lie is a counterfeit truth and is best exposed by concentrated exposure to the truth.

step three | **Living Out Your Core Beliefs**

Information that leads to transformation requires action. Turning a belief into a lived out core value requires that intentional actions be carried out consistently over time. The result will be change that can be experienced by the people around you. Use the following questions as tools to turn your beliefs into intentional actions that you consistently do over time:

— What will you do differently today to demonstrate your beliefs?

— Are there declarations you could make daily that strengthen your belief? Which ones will you use?

— What Scriptures could you meditate on?

— Who can you ask about how your beliefs are being experienced by those around you? Is there someone in your life who will give you feedback and hold you accountable?

— What other resources can you get to listen to, read, watch or use, that will strengthen your core beliefs?

— How can you keep your beliefs at the front of your mind throughout the day until they are lived out?

We encourage you to take at least one of the above questions and turn it into a daily intentional action. Do this purposefully for 21 days to build a new habit. This will in turn reinforce your belief until it becomes a lived out core value – a foundation for building a lifestyle that results in dreams consistently being realized.

setting yourself up to succeed

If I had eight hours to chop down a tree,
I'd spend six hours sharpening my ax.

- Abraham Lincoln

Many people start on the journey of living their dreams, but some turn back due to the cost, the challenge or the obstacles they face. Some were simply ill prepared for the journey.

So, what are some vital keys or tools you'll need to prepare for your journey? What has helped others succeed in their journey?

In this chapter, we offer you three keys that will help make your journey successful: Daily dream thoughts, daily dream goals, and the power of a relationship with a Dream Friend or Dream Partner.

For as he thinks in his heart, so is he.

Proverbs 23:7a

daily dream thoughts

Our lives become a reflection of what we think about most often. Regardless of what we may say, it is really what we believe in our heart that determines our course, the decisions we make and defines what we become. If you think something is impossible, you will never try it. But if you believe something is possible, you will come up with creative ways to make something happen. The Old Testament gives the account of twelve Israelite spies who went into their promised land. Ten came back with a positive report of the land, but also a fearful, negative report of the people who live there, saying, *"...we were like grasshoppers in our own sight, and so we were in their sight"* (Numbers 13:33b). The way they saw themselves was how they imagined other people saw them. Viewing themselves through fear cost them their lives as well as the lives of an entire generation of Israelites in the desert.

How we think about ourselves is very important. Positive beliefs can equip us to realize our dreams and also help those in our

The result of a transformed mind is that the impossible becomes logical.

- Bill Johnson

realm of influence to live out their dreams. Poor thinking not only keeps you from realizing your dreams, but it can significantly cost your children, your friends and your community. Much of what Jesus did and taught was offered to change the way we think about who God is, what He is really like, and about who we are in relationship to Him. We are His children, lovingly made in His image and likeness. As His children we have access to everything we need to live fully alive. With Him nothing is impossible. What does your life say you believe to be true about God? What does your life say you believe to be true about yourself? What are you thinking?

In order to build a lifestyle of successfully pursuing your dreams, you need to have right thinking. It's important to have the right thoughts or beliefs about God, yourself and others. You can keep your dreams alive by upholding that right thinking. Whatever you think about grows. Thinking daily dream thoughts helps keep

Take the first step in faith.

You don't have to see the

whole staircase. Just take

the first step.

- Martin Luther King Jr.

your focus on your Dream Journey. It also helps you maintain alertness to opportunities. When you are intentionally looking for something, you will be more likely to recognize it when it crosses your path.

daily dream goals

At the end of one of my coaching sessions with a young Dreamer in the seventh grade, he made the profound statement, *"I've learned that anything is possible, I just have to build myself up for it."* He was talking about breaking big dreams or big goals down into small, seemingly insignificant steps that suddenly come together to accomplish the dream.

Daily dream goals are those things you act on that move you closer to the dream each day. Thoughts are great for keeping the vision in front of you and maintaining focus, but it is the action you take that will actually get you to where you want to go. We have a bulletin board in our home and on it is a bright piece of paper that states, *"What am I doing today to walk toward my dream?"* It's a constant reminder for us to make choices about protecting our priorities and doing something, however small, each day that moves us closer to achieving our dreams.

A knife cuts because of focus.

It's easy to get caught up with the busyness of life and spend weeks on end without making any progress toward your dream. Daily or even weekly Dream Goals help keep a reminder in front of us to continue advancing. At the beginning of the week, I put on my task list the things that I don't want overlooked in the busyness of my life. It might be the book I want to finish, the person I want to meet or the resource I want to locate. I find that when I make a commitment to actively pursue something each week, even if it seems insignificant, I continue building momentum and keep the passion for the dream inside me alive.

dream friend or dream partner (what do i look for?)

All through this book we continue to emphasize the importance of relationship and community; the brother who was born to walk with us through adversity (*see* Proverbs 17:17); the friend who sticks closer than a brother (*see* Proverbs 18:24); the threefold cord that is not easily broken (*see* Ecclesiastes 4:12). If you gain nothing else from this book, gain the importance of covenant community that results in great power and great grace like that shown in Acts 4:32. A Dream Culture is one full of powerful relationships, where the impossible becomes logical.

We believe that one of the most significant factors in the successful pursuit of a dream is having a powerful relationship with another person who can hold you accountable to your greatness and walk with you on the journey. We call this person a Dream Friend or a Dream Partner.

So, could anybody be a suitable Dream Partner? Joseph, in Genesis 37, found out the hard way that sharing your dream with some people can result in them wanting to kill you. Choose wisely, as many a person has had their dream crushed by a well-meaning friend who wanted to save them from disappointment. No friend is immune to this feeling, especially when it concerns someone you deeply care about and don't want to see suffer pain.

I have a friend who decided to give up a perfectly good career as an occupational therapist in order to pursue her dream of becoming a pilot with a commercial license. To be honest, when she first told me what she was going to do, I had some serious

reservations. My heart for my friend's welfare made me want to advise her to drop the whole crazy idea and play it safe. I saw the potential for financial ruin as well as other pitfalls that might await her on her journey to become a commercial pilot. I wanted to rescue her from them all. Thankfully, I kept my mouth shut!

> *Keep away from people who try to belittle your ambition.*
>
> *Small people always do that.*
>
> *But the really great make you feel that you, too, can become great.*
>
> *- Mark Twain*

Three years later, my friend graduated from pilot school, was accepted into Missionary Aviation Fellowship and was assigned to fly heavenly missions into Papua New Guinea. All that to say, those closest to you may *love* you too much to encourage you to take your biggest risks because they want you to stay safe.

It is amazing how God, who *is* love, encourages us to take risks beyond ourselves and promises us He will never leave our side. He is the greatest Dream Partner of all! What would it be like if we could imitate Him for our friends and their dreams?

When choosing someone to be a Dream Partner, look for someone who believes in you and for someone who believes that the impossible is not only possible but also highly likely when God is involved.

Choose someone that will have the courage to ask you the tough questions about how you are doing with what you said you were going to do. In order to do this, they need to be part of your life on a regular basis. With the communication technology we have access to, a Dream Partner who is helping you stay focused on losing weight could be on the other side of the world; but in reality, someone you attend the gym with on a daily basis may be a better choice.

Who do you have in your life right now that you could build relationship with in order to form a growth-centered partnership, one where you can commit to one another's personal growth and development?

What would it take for you to become vulnerable enough to not only share your own heart dreams, but also the personal challenges you need help overcoming in order to achieve those dreams?

Now, who in your life can you help to champion their dreams?

I am a success today because I had a friend who believed in me and I didn't have the heart to let him down...

~ President Abraham Lincoln

dream activation exercise

step one | **Dream Champions**

There are people all around you who are already living some aspect of their dream. They know what it is to overcome the challenges and pressures that keep them from intentionally living their dreams. More often than not, they are more than willing to share their journey with you and, in doing so, encourage and inspire you on your own journey.

— Who do you know who is living their dream?

— How did they discover their dream?

— How did they begin to walk it out?

— What would it take for you to meet with them and ask them their story of discovery and pursuit of their dream?

Check out www.roadtripnation.com for some great ideas, inspirations, and interviews with people from all walks of life who share their stories.

step two | **Dream Friend or Dream Partner**

If you haven't done so already, now is a great time to set up an intentional relationship with someone who holds you accountable to your greatness.

— Who do you have around you right now who believes in you and would hold you accountable to your dreams?

— When could you meet with them to discuss partnering for the purpose of helping each other achieve your dreams?

— Make a commitment to inspire and encourage one another in taking steps towards reaching your dreams.

putting legs on your dreams

...faith without works is dead.

James 2:20

By this point in your Dream Journey you will have unlocked some dreams and have them written down. That's the first step to unleashing you as a Dreamer and launching your dreams on the journey towards reality. Now we're ready to put some legs on those dreams. This is where it gets really practical and you have to do things. *You* are responsible for *you!*

In this chapter we will give you some concepts and basic coaching tools that you can use along with the Holy Spirit and a Dream Friend. We can't emphasize enough the importance of inviting the Holy Spirit on the journey with you, and also the importance of having a Dream Friend or Dream Partner who is committed to seeing you become who you were designed to be… fully alive.

Nothing happens outside of growth-centered relationships.

Heaven is founded on relationship (a Father, a Son, and the Holy Spirit). Earth was created from that relationship with relationship in mind. We were not created to be independent individuals living in our own little spheres. Rather, we are inter-dependent beings, living and creating from community. It is that community that brings multi-dimensional perspective and encouragement, inflow and outflow, accountability and significance, and that results in never-ending increase.

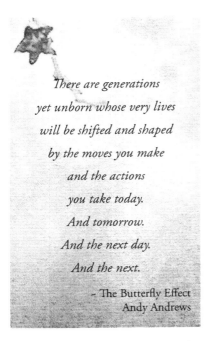

There are generations yet unborn whose very lives will be shifted and shaped by the moves you make and the actions you take today. And tomorrow. And the next day. And the next.

– The Butterfly Effect Andy Andrews

The following coaching concepts and tools are primarily taken from the book, *Coaching Questions,* by Tony Stoltzfus. This book is full of powerful questions, keys, examples and exercises that you can use in questioning yourself and others. If you want to further develop your ability to ask yourself the right questions and help those around you gain traction toward realizing their dreams, we highly recommend you get a copy.

which dream do i start with?

You may now be staring at a list of 100 dreams. Wow, what a list! What do your dreams say about you? What are the themes that are consistently represented through them? How do you know which one to start with? Here's another great opportunity to ask the Holy Spirit for advice. He gives wisdom freely to those who ask and is amazing at highlighting things we wouldn't always think of. This journey is as much a journey of growing in relationship with Him, as it is a roadmap to achieving your dreams with Him. Your Dream List is like an invitation into His heart for you; like road markers into the heart of God.

Some questions you can ask yourself to help you decide which dream to start with include:

- *Which dream do I feel motivated to do something about right now?*
- *What dream do I feel life on when I think about it?*
- *What dream am I working on already?*
- *What dream is currently surrounded by some beneficial situation or circumstance that would lend me momentum to go after it right now?*

Or, if you really dare...

- *What dream am I most afraid of?*

Remember, you already have what it takes to get started. God's divine power has given us all things that pertain to life and godliness (*see* II Peter 1:3). This means you already have, at least in seed form, all that you need to become who He has called you to be. You only need to find the seed that is already in your hand.

Keep yourself focused on what you *do* have, rather than what you don't have. It is amazing how when we trust God and believe nothing is impossible, creative thoughts are released to establish the *how-to* of going after your dream.

When NASA launched the first mission to the moon, they first had to believe that space travel and landing on the moon was possible. Without that belief, nothing would have happened. Believing involves action. Belief is like the thermostat in your life, setting the climate for your outcomes. Negative belief, or unbelief, results in the lack of growth or the absence of positive action. Unbelief will leave you with a wish list of unfulfilled dreams. On the contrary, belief will result in confirming action steps that will create momentum and forward movement toward the realization of your dreams.

The Process of Putting Legs on Your Dreams

Once you've decided on the dream that you want to pursue first, the next process is one that you can use over and over again to develop successive steps to walk out your dream. The questioning, or *coaching*, process helps turn the dream into a goal, and then into an action step. The action step leads to an outcome that can be reviewed in light of the goal and the overall dream (*see diagram*). Successive goals can then be made or adjusted to continue the journey towards the fulfillment of the dream.

the coaching funnel

The Coaching Funnel is a visual representation of the coaching process by which we turn a dream into a specific goal, then explore the situation and develop options from which we determine an action step.

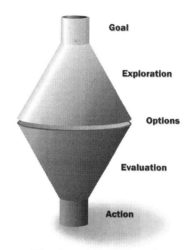

The Coaching Funnel

Once the goal is established, questions are used to fully explore what is going on in the situation before jumping to options and actions. This is called *widening* the funnel, and will allow you to get more information and understanding out on the table before generating solutions.

Following this, the questions become more specific as options are evaluated and then a particular action step is identified. The specific action step, or steps, will then accomplish the goal and move you forward on your dream journey.

(Used by permission, T. Stoltzfus, *Coaching Questions*)

STEP ONE
turning your dream into a goal (focus)

The first step is narrowing your unlimited dream into a defined goal. You may find that your dream will need to be broken down into a number of successive goals. While a dream is unlimited, a goal is a one-sentence statement that clearly defines what you want to achieve by a certain time or date.

The S.M.A.R.T. format (Specific, Measurable, Attainable, Relevant and Time-specific) is a useful tool to help develop this statement. The goal brings focus. Without it, the dream can remain somewhat elusive, making it difficult to define clear action steps. A goal is a specific, declared, future objective that you are committed to reaching. The key to developing a goal quickly is to stay focused only on *where* you want to go and not *how* to get there until after the goal is set.

Following are some helpful questions under each category of the S.M.A.R.T. goal format, including a good and bad example for each.

 Specific : You can state clearly where you are going.

- What will this dream look like when accomplished?
- What has to be done to achieve this dream?
- What do you need to be in order to achieve this dream?
- What else can you tell me about it in order to be more specific?

- What will be different when you have accomplished this dream?

- How could you define this more clearly or in fewer words?

Bad Example : Write a book

Good example : Write a book that inspires and empowers young and old in the church community to dream.

Measurable : You've included a way to measure progress.

- How can you quantify this goal (put it into a measure or number) so we will know when you've accomplished it?

- How will you or others know you have achieved progress on this goal?

- You said, "Inspires and empowers." Define what you mean by that.

Bad Example : Write a book that inspires and empowers.

Good example : Write a book by December 2010.

Attainable : It is within your capabilities and depends only on you.

- Does this goal depend on anyone else's choices?

- Is this goal within your capabilities?

- Are there any barriers or circumstances that are working against you achieving this goal?

- How could you rewrite this S.M.A.R.T. goal so it depends only on you?

Bad Example : Sell 100,000 copies of the book.

Good Example : Introduce the book to 12 different marketing and distribution networks by the end of 2011

Note: Attainable can include the faith factor combined with your actions, but should not be dependent on the responses or actions of other people. For example, I cannot determine whether 100,000 people will buy the book, but I can introduce the book to multiple marketing and distribution networks and pray favor and an unusual advantage over book sales.

R **Relevant** : You care enough about this goal to make it a priority

- What makes this important to you?
- What things are you prepared to put aside in order to make this goal happen?
- On a scale of one to ten, how important is it that you reach this goal?
- If you didn't achieve this goal, how would you feel?

For example: I was coaching an individual who wanted to start a business and had three different business options in front of him. Initially, he was planning to explore all three opportunities, but when I asked him to tell me, on a scale of one to ten how each of these fit with his passion and purpose, he immediately gave two options a zero out of ten and one an eleven out of ten! The goal then became to develop a business plan for the remaining opportunity that had all the relevance and resulting motivation.

Time-Specific : It has a deadline or target completion date.

- When will you reach this goal?
- When will this be an established habit?
- When will you start this?
- What is your targeted completion date?

Bad Example : Write a book this year

Good Example : Starting next month, write one chapter per month to have the book completed for the printer by December 2010.

Once you have developed a one-sentence statement of your goal, write it down. Your goal should clearly state the objective you want to reach by a particular date. This will keep you focused in the process of developing action steps, reviewing the outcomes, and then continuing the process as your dream materializes right before your eyes.

STEP TWO
exploring the goal

The second step involves fully exploring the goal (or the dream behind it), what led up to it, and what is going on under the surface, in your heart. This takes the focus from the goal itself to the situation surrounding the goal. It widens the perspective, as in the image of the coaching funnel, to give the bigger picture or underlying factors. Exploration can involve probing the external situation and the internal responses that you may be having to the situation. This is where the real depth of your heart's desires, motivations and beliefs become apparent allowing you to more clearly decide on options to proceed.

Following are some questions to ask yourself or get your Dream Friend or Dream Partner to ask you. Look for repeated words, or words showing the evidence of emotion, and the tone of voice as you listen for the heart:

- What is the background leading up to this goal?
- Tell me more.
- What is behind that?
- Where do you see this going? What will that look like?
- Where else in your life is this evident?
- What is going on inside you when you consider this situation?
- Tell me more.
- What are the most important factors or players in this situation?
- What is most significant for you?

It is common at this stage of the Coaching Funnel to uncover deeper, driving passions or emotions and sometimes and even an "aha" moment where you begin to tap a hidden heart desire or motivation that you didn't even realize was there.

Recently, I was coaching a person who had a dream to establish a life coaching business. As we explored the dream, using some of the questions above, we uncovered that the desire was motivated out of this person's history of gaining freedom from abuse. It was a significant discovery. The deepest desire was to coach people with similar backgrounds into their own personal freedom. If we had not first explored the situation, we would not have tapped into that level of motivation or the specific focus that the business was to have.

Once you feel you have fully explored the situation surrounding the goal, it is time to develop some possible options to proceed.

STEP THREE
developing options - what could you do?

Now is the time to think creatively to develop multiple potential solutions to reach the goal. Often you will easily list several ideas that you have previously considered. The process becomes powerful when you push beyond these initial ideas, beyond the box, to discover options that you hadn't previously considered.

The following are some questions to help you discover options. Be encouraged to continue to explore and uncover options beyond the immediate and obvious:

- What could you do to move yourself toward your goal?

- What other options could you think of?

- If you imagined yourself in someone else's shoes, what other options might they come up with?

- Let's shoot for at least five possible options. What else could you do?

- What obstacles might keep you from reaching your goal? How could you remove them?

- What have you done in similar situations in the past?
- If you asked the Holy Spirit, what would He suggest?

Pausing to consider some of these questions, especially in the presence of a friend or in your own quiet time, will release creativity to unlock seemingly hidden options. Our God is the God of Creation, and we are made in His image. We have the ability to tap into creative thought and access realms with unlimited wisdom, revelation and understanding.

I had an amusing situation of this happen when I was giving an example of what this looks like in my own life. As I was explaining the process to a friend and giving him an example of listing different options for a goal I had, I blurted out an option that I hadn't even consciously thought of. I suddenly paused, looked at my friend, and said, *"Wow, I'm going to do just that!"* The resulting action step was significant in obtaining favor and advice to move me toward the accomplishment of one of my dreams.

STEP FOUR
deciding on an option to pursue - what will you do?

Now it's time to decide which option, or options, you will pursue that can move you toward your goal. Options are what you *could* do. Of these options, some of them you will *want* to do. This part of the process is about turning choice into action by clarifying what you *will* do.

- The options you mentioned are [*read back through the list of options that were listed in the previous step*]: What stands out to you in that list?
- Which options do you want to pursue?

- Which of these options will most effectively move you toward your goal?

- What are the advantages and disadvantages of each option?

- What is the best option?

STEP FIVE
action - making it happen

Finally, it's simply time to just get it done. Here we turn the option that you have decided on into concrete steps with high buy-in. Clearly stating what you will do creates both commitment and accountability.

- Let's turn that into an action step. What exactly will you do?

- What will you do and by when?

- You mentioned that you (could, should, might, ought to) do _____. What will you commit to doing?

- Is that a realistic timetable? Are there any other obstacles we need to address before you move forward on this step?

Hope brings life. But in order to attain victory, hope must be accompanied by action. The dream that you have will remain a dream unless you make a conscious decision to turn it into tangible steps that you can walk out.

Well done is better than well said.

~ Benjamin Franklin

Graveyards all around the world are full of buried dreams. You can choose to take the steps that will turn your dreams into a reality. The choice is yours.

Now may the God of hope fill you
with all joy and peace believing,
that you may abound in hope
by the power of the Holy Spirit.

Romans 15:13

And God is able to make all grace
abound toward you, that you,
always having all sufficiency in all things,
may have an abundance for every good work.

II Corinthians 9:8

 *dream activation exercise*

step one | **Identify a Dream to Begin With**

Take your Dream List in your hand and close your eyes for a moment. Ask the Holy Spirit to help you identify a dream to start acting on. Now, run your eyes over your list and take note of which dream stands out to you.

— Which dream do you feel strongly motivated to do something about right now?

— Which dream would be easy to act on right now?

— What future dream could you start working on now to prepare or position yourself to fulfill?

— Which dream is God breathing on in this season of your life?

Write this dream down and then take some time to imagine what it would look and feel like when this dream is accomplished.

— How will your life be different? How will that feel?

— As you imagine living this dream, what sights, smells, sounds and sensations are you aware of?

— Now consider the people around you, your friends, family, colleagues and community. How could achieving this dream affect their lives?

step two | **Follow the S.M.A.R.T. Goal Process**

Now take the dream you have chosen and follow the S.M.A.R.T. goal process to turn that dream into a goal statement. This would be a great time to work with your Dream Friend or Dream Partner, who could help you with these questions and keep you accountable to the action steps you decide on. Write down a clear, obtainable, time-oriented goal statement that you will act on.

Specific, **M**easurable, **A**ttainable, **R**elevant, **T**ime-specific

You may want to refer to the questions and examples in this chapter that walk you through the S.M.A.R.T. goal process.

step three | **Turn the Goal Into an Action**

Now follow steps two through five in the Coaching Funnel outlined in this chapter:

— Explore your goal.

— Develop options.

— Decide which options to act on.

— Make concrete steps to accomplish them.

You can follow this process again and again to activate different dreams and also activate the dreams of others.

You may want to refer to the questions at each section to help clarify the process.

faith and action

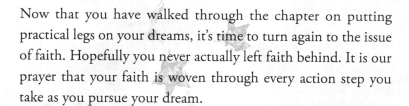

For with God nothing will be impossible.

Luke 1:37

Now that you have walked through the chapter on putting practical legs on your dreams, it's time to turn again to the issue of faith. Hopefully you never actually left faith behind. It is our prayer that your faith is woven through every action step you take as you pursue your dream.

Our desire is that you pray and get Heaven's perspective at each stage of your dream, and hear God's voice leading you at every point. His grace is available to you in the pursuit of your dreams, but it is easy for us to get so practical that we think we can do it all in our own strength. We encourage you to keep connected to God throughout the process, so that achieving your dreams does not become an end in itself, but rather an expression of your pursuit of Him and what He has for you. This means constantly talking to Him about your dreams, and including him in the planning.

You are partners with Him in your life journey, and partnership requires great communication. You both bring something to the partnership and it is important that you know what is your part, and what is God's part.

Every person in a successful partnership has a clear understanding of his or her responsibilities. A business partnership where both partners assume responsibility for the finances of the company, but neither one of them take responsibility for selling anything, would soon fall apart. For each dream you need to have a clear understanding of what your responsibility is, and what you believe God will do on your behalf.

The previous chapter focused on your part of the equation. By now you have probably started to take action steps toward seeing your dream realized. You will need to continue to push forward in order to take new ground, and you will also need to adjust your course in order to stay on track. In the midst of this, we encourage you to keep seeking His perspective on your progress and allow Jesus to speak to you about mid-course changes of direction. Remember, this is part of your journey to discover more of who He is and who He has created you to be. Often, we don't have a complete picture of where we are heading before we set out, so we must seek His guidance to keep us heading in the right direction.

In this chapter, we want to spend a little time talking about how to understand God's side of the partnership. God makes a great partner. He is faithful and can be trusted to do what He says He will do. He will never let you down and He has more resources and wisdom than you do. The trouble is that many people never tap into the resources He wants to make available to them because they lack understanding of how to partner with Him. Partnering with God means walking in faith.

faith is the evidence of hope

The Bible says that without faith it is impossible to please God (*see* Hebrews 11:6). That's a huge statement! It means that faith is the non-negotiable currency that God looks for in His interaction with you.

If faith is such a big deal to God, we had better know what faith is. According to Hebrews 11:1, *"...faith is the substance of things hoped for, the evidence of things not seen."* Faith is described here by two very solid words—substance and evidence. Usually these words are reserved for things that you can see, taste, and feel, but here they are used to describe faith. In a court of law the judge is unlikely to accept your faith as evidence, but God has a different standard. He says it is faith that pleases Him, and His description of faith has substance!

DREAMS ACCELERATED BY HEAVEN

Jake and his wife's number one **dream was to buy their own home.** In coming to his first meeting, Jake's Dream Coach asked the Holy Spirit for a specific word to encourage Jake. All he heard was the word "proceed." This sounded a little unusual until they started talking. It turned out that Jake was looking at a promising house to buy **but he just wasn't sure if it was the right one.**

On hearing the word from the Dream Coach, the level of excitement and courage in the room dramatically increased. Here's what happened next:

"Last year, we didn't qualify for the loan we wanted. This year, our finances have not changed, but we qualified for the loan. We thought we would need to borrow the deposit from our family. However, we found a bank-owned house that only needed a deposit of $1,000, so no family loan was needed. The house previously sold for $280,000, and the bank was now asking $166,000. We offered $150,000 and it was accepted! Initially, we were shown that the property was half an acre, but after our offer was accepted and checking the title, we found that it was double that! What was impossible three months ago happened in just weeks. Everything feels more attainable. It has shifted my timetable of what to expect, what is possible now."

So what *is* faith? Faith is that thing inside of you that allows you to go from just hoping that something will happen, to *knowing* it will happen. When you have faith, you will "go to the bank" on it. Abraham's faith was credited to him as righteousness because he ignored his natural circumstances and just trusted God that He would do what He said He would do. The Hebrews 11 *"Hall of Fame"* lists many great men and women of faith. These generals of faith took what God said as solid *substance* they could count on, even though their natural eyes could not yet see it.

Faith is the thing that empowers you to make declarations with your words that create something from nothing. As Hebrews 11:3 states, *"By faith we understand that the worlds were framed by the word of God, so that the things which are seen were not made of things which are visible."* God made something from nothing through His words; you were created in His image and His likeness. You get to do the same... by faith.

partnering with God involves us walking in faith

Partnering with God involves walking in faith. In order to see our God-given dreams realized, we must know how to see with the eyes of faith and walk according to what we see with those eyes, rather than our natural eyes. We believe this involves two arenas. The first is in our action steps – the "us" side of the partnership. As previously stated, just because we are doing something, does not mean that we abandon faith and do it in our own strength. We are wise if we partner faith with our action and believe God will supernaturally increase our efforts to bring more fruit than we would otherwise expect.

The second arena where we must employ faith is in the God side of the partnership. This may seem obvious, but we have seen many people trip up on this point. As people look at their dreams, they have a tendency to classify them as those they have the ability to achieve through hard work, and those that they need God to do for them. In the S.M.A.R.T. goal format, this is wise. It allows us to clearly take ownership of the things that are under our control and not expend all of our energy stressing about what we cannot control. However, the down side of this for many people is that it allows us to mentally put those things in a category where we have no responsibility and no control over the outcome. In this place, we become passive and feel powerless and move from faith to unbelief.

Let me give you an example to help explain what I mean. Let's say that Jane has a dream to get married. This is a great dream. She has put it into the arena of God's side of the partnership, because she believes He has the perfect man for her and she is unable to make it happen through her own strength. This is wise, as many have felt the pain of trying to make this dream happen through their own ability. The problem is that it then becomes easy for Jane to begin to think there is nothing she can do to sow into that dream. This is not true. It is not a case of sitting back and just waiting for God to do His thing and becoming passive. Jane still has much she can do to sow into her dream of getting married while still leaving the outcome totally to God.

First, she can position herself to stay in a posture of faith over this matter. That might mean regular prayer times, thanking God for her spouse and praying for her future husband. It might be making declarations over herself or using her sanctified imagination to picture the day when her dream will be fulfilled. One response is passive; one is active. The first response brings a feeling of powerlessness, but the second keeps Jane actively sowing into her dream, yet trusting God for the outcome.

Beyond intentionally keeping faith alive to believe God for her dream of being married to come true, Jane may also choose to take some other action steps to sow into that dream. These faith action steps will partner with what God is doing on her behalf to move her toward the dream. One young lady I worked with realized that although she had a dream to get married, she rarely made any effort to get to know anyone outside her immediate world. She chose to make a goal around intentionally meeting new people (male and female) to grow in her ability to be a friend. This was not taking over God's part of the process, but was partnering with Him by putting her faith into action.

The book of James has a lot to say about faith. Chapter one starts off by saying that faith needs to be without doubting. The emphasis in this chapter is on the level of belief. James gives a vivid, visual picture to show that having faith, and yet not really believing, is like a wave on the sea tossed by the wind. He then goes on to explain that if you are double-minded you should not expect you will receive anything from the Lord! Wow, he makes a good case for having faith that doesn't waver.

In chapter two, James moves on to another aspect of faith. He takes the requirement from just believing and makes it clear that faith needs to be accompanied by action.

What does it profit, my brethren, if someone says he has faith but does not have works? Can faith save him? If a brother or sister is naked and destitute of daily food, and one of you says to them, "Depart in peace, be warmed and filled," but you do not give them the things which are needed for the body, what does it profit? Thus also faith by itself, if it does not have works, is dead. But someone will say, "You have faith, and I have works." Show me your faith without your works, and I will show you my faith by my works. You believe that there is one God. You do well. Even the demons believe — and tremble! But do you want to know, O foolish man, that faith without works is dead?

Was not Abraham our father justified by works when he offered Isaac his son on the altar? Do you see that faith was working together with his works, and by works faith was made perfect? And the Scripture was fulfilled which says, "Abraham believed God, and it was accounted to him for righteousness." And he was called the friend of God.

You see then that a man is justified by works, and not by faith only. Likewise, was not Rahab the harlot also justified by works when she received the messengers and sent them out another way? For as the body without the spirit is dead, so faith without works is dead also.

James 2:14 - 26

The above passage closely links faith and action. James says that faith is shown *by* our works. Here he is not talking about works by themselves, but works linked with faith. He is saying that our actions demonstrate the faith we have in our heart. It is not our

108

works that save us. It is faith (*see* Ephesians 2:8-9). But God is interested in our actions in response to His voice. My life is a result of the decisions I have made and the actions I have taken as a result of those decisions. How I live shows what I really believe (faith or unbelief). It is easy to say that I trust God to provide for me, but if I am constantly stressed out over money, my life says that I don't trust Him. Our lives trumpet the sound of what we really believe.

Abraham's action of putting Isaac on the altar was a natural outcome of the things he believed (his faith) and so it was credited to him for righteousness. (*See* Genesis 22:1-19). And so it is for you. God is looking to see what you do with what He says to you. In the example above, Jane had a desire to get married. She made a decision to partner with God in order to move toward the dream. But her decision to walk in faith in going after the dream will be shown by action, in response to God's voice.

The same is true for you. It is great to have dreams that require God to show up. Your dreams should be so big that they scare you. But even for those dreams that are beyond what you can control, you have a part to play in them. You can attract breakthrough by positioning yourself to receive from God. In his book, *Face to Face With God,* Bill Johnson gives keys for how to "set up an ambush" so that you are in God's firing line for blessing (*see Face to Face With God,* chapter six, *Setting Up An Ambush*). You can't control God, but you can look for what He loves and what He responds to and align yourself with that.

Our heart is that you will learn to sow into even those dreams that are in God's hands in a way that says, *"I know I can't make this happen, but I'm going to make sure that I am doing what I can to position, propel or prepare myself for it."*

Let me finish with another example. Let's say I have a dream to see thousands of people healed through my ministry. As I put that dream into a S.M.A.R.T. goal, I realize that I have no control whether or not people will get healed. As a result, I change the S.M.A.R.T. goal to: *"I will pray for 1,000 people for healing within a year."* My goal now fits the S.M.A.R.T. goal format, because it is specific, measurable, attainable (dependant only on me), realistic, and time-bound. This is great. It allows me to focus on my side of the partnership and leave the outcome of whether the people get healed in God's arena.

The problem is that there is the potential for me to move into passivity over God's side of the equation rather than looking at

Our lives trumpet the sound of what we really believe

what I can do to position myself to increase in favor with God. Passivity looks like simply praying for people in faith and just asking God to, *"bless me and grow me in seeing people healed."* This will attract a measure of favor as you align yourself with God's heart to see people healed, and as you take the risk to step out in faith.

However, there is a greater level of engaging with this dream. The first part still looks the same. My S.M.A.R.T. goal remains to pray for 1,000 people in the next year. But as I recognize that my faith is what moves God, I am also interacting with Him over His side of the partnership. It may be that I undertake some training in healing prayer. It may be that I consciously choose to step out of my comfort zone in other areas to grow in my capacity to move in faith. I may intentionally grow friendships with people who move strongly in faith or choose to serve in a ministry where praying for healing happens regularly. All of these steps help me take ownership of my growth without trying to do what only God can do.

Taking action steps to pursue growing in dreams like these keeps the ball in my court. God still determines whether or not the dream is fulfilled, but I have partnered my faith with action to do all that I can. The goal here is not just mere activity, but taking an active stance on what could easily be seen as something outside of my control. Sometimes the active stance will be to do nothing but trust, to simply stand and see the Lord come through for you. But if He is asking you to stand, you are in a posture of responsibility rather than a posture of powerlessness.

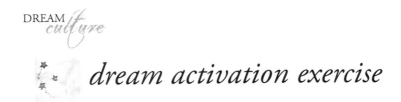

dream activation exercise

Adding the Faith Dimension: The Art of Thinking Bigger

step one | **Choose A Dream**

Find a dream from your Dream Cache that you think might be too small, or where you were too afraid to really write down what you were thinking.

step two | **Dream Bigger**

Now, on your own or with a friend, increase the size of that dream beyond the borders of your comfort zone. Visualize what it would be like if you made your dream ten times bigger, added bells and whistles, multiplied its impact and shot for the moon.

It doesn't matter whether or not what you visualize feels realistic or possible to you – the purpose of this exercise is to stretch your dreaming muscles and learn to think beyond your limitations.

You don't have to commit to this larger dream yet – just practice the skill of dreaming big... just like your Father in Heaven.

Here are some questions to help:

— How would this dream look if it were 10 times bigger? What if it were a hundred times bigger?

— If God went before you and eliminated all the obstacles, what could this dream possibly become?

— What other areas of influence could this dream expand into?

— If you were fearless, what would you attempt?

If God is your God, dream big.

D. L. Moody

There is more of God beyond your fingertips.

are you really ready for this?

For which of you, intending to build a tower, does not sit down first and count the cost, whether he has enough to finish it...

Jesus Christ, Luke 14:28

By now, most people are really energized about going after their dreams. But do you really have what it takes to make them reality? How can we prepare you for the journey so that you succeed, so that you finish strong? The next couple of sections are about some of the key attitudes and mindsets that you need to have or overcome in order to successfully navigate the journey. In addition to this, a great resource that specifically asks ten questions to help you *"see it and seize it"* is, *Put Your Dream to the Test,* by John Maxwell.

ownership

So what kind of mindset do we need to have when it comes to pursuing our dreams? The first thing is to take ownership. You

are the only one who is responsible to make your dreams come true. There will be people along the way, people who lend you their faith or courage when yours needs a boost. There may be people who support you financially, provide other resources, or connect you to others who can get you where you need to go. But in the end, your dream is *your* dream and you have to really *own* it in order to bring it to pass. As we work with people as their Dream Coach, we hear many amazing dreams. All of them have value, but sadly not all of them will come to pass. We have come to realize that the responsibility for managing the dreams of others or making their dream come true is not ours.

We do all that we can to encourage, stimulate thinking or troubleshoot problems with a Dreamer, but in the end the dream is still *their dream.* The Dream Coach (or parent, leader, friend or spouse) cannot own another person's dream and sadly if the Dreamer does not take ownership, it will never become reality.

In attaining any significant dream, there is almost always pain and cost at some point along the way. (*Those of us who have given birth can well attest to this fact!*) So, what is it that takes you past the point of pain? Self-discipline will take you some of the way. Determination will take you so far, but will eventually run out. Encouragement from others will help you get past some of the obstacles and challenges. Even a supernatural cloud by day and a fire by night will not do for you what only you can do for yourself.

What is it that will take you to the point of pain and beyond in pursuit of the dream? It is *ownership*, the mindset that says, *"This thing belongs to me and I am willing to pay for it!"* When you link that kind of mindset with the truth that pursuing the dream is a

God-given mandate, you have a compelling reason not to give up.

So how do you know if you truly own your dream? Are you willing to pay the price to bring it to pass? Are you ready to commit energy, time and resources to pursue the dream? If no one else joins or supports you, will you still pursue it? What would it take for you to let it go or replace it with something else? The answers to these questions give an indication of how much you own your dream.

THERE IS MORE!

Robbie was a stay-at-home mom and wife of 33 years to Mike, a highly successful businessman. Her *"impossible"* dream was to be a partner in her husband's business, traveling and speaking alongside him. After attending a Dream Presentation, she finally spoke out her dream and wrote it down as something she wanted to go after.

Initially Robbie didn't really believe that it could happen, but she approached her husband and began to talk to him about her desire to work with him. His first response was not encouraging. After showing no interest in the business for years it was hard for her husband to believe that she was serious. But Robbie persevered: *"It wasn't easy. Mike and I had many discussions about what this would look like and why I wanted to do this. The best thing was that both of us were coming clean on things we had ignored for years but were so important for us living and working as one."*

It took a lot of discussion and a willingness to face the internal barriers to making this work, but Mike and Robbie have now started on a whole new journey of life together. Beyond 33 years of marriage and a highly influential and successful business career, they have discovered that **there is more.** Together, they birthed *Frank Consulting*, and partnership has taken on a whole new meaning.

s

motivation

> *People often say that motivation doesn't last.*
> *Well, neither does bathing – That's why we recommend it daily.*

> ~ Zig Ziglar

For all of us, there are easy days and tough days on the journey to fulfilling a dream. There are days when I don't feel highly motivated and would rather not pay the price to see my big dream fulfilled. Like you, every day I get to choose whether I will pursue the little dreams or the big dreams that God has placed in my heart. So what is it that compels me to go on? Why do I keep going even when the going gets tough?

In order to answer that question, we first have to ask ourselves why we had the dream in the first place. How is that dream a reflection of my values, attitudes and passions? When we can lock into the passion behind the dream, we will have the energy to pursue the dream even when the going gets tough. When the dream is initially ignited inside of us, we feel the rush of enthusiasm and excitement as we consider what it would look like to live the dream. That enthusiasm takes us through the first steps as we begin to make progress toward the dream's fulfillment. But for all of us, there comes a point on the journey where we find out just how motivated we are to fulfill the dream. At that moment, as the difficulties that must be overcome move clearly

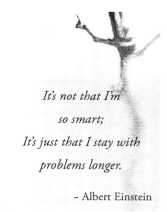

It's not that I'm
so smart;
It's just that I stay with
problems longer.

~ Albert Einstein

into view, we become aware of the cost of the journey and we make the decision whether to go on in pursuit of the dream, or to abandon our quest. How you respond to this moment will determine the outcome of the dream.

There are always at least *three options* in response to this crossroad. The first option is to *abandon the dream altogether.* It may be that this is the best option. Perhaps the dream was not what you expected, or the price really is too high. Be willing to search your heart and motives and count the cost. Was this your dream in the first place? Do you own it? How important is it to you in light of the new developments? Is it God's timing to go after it? Don't quickly abandon your dream at the first sign of trouble, because a dream worth living is a dream worth fighting for, but do be willing to ask yourself the hard questions.

Having asked yourself these questions and having decided to continue the dream, the next option is to *modify the dream and eliminate the obstacles by changing the goal.* This may be a great option if you had set your initial goal too high or the dream was not realistic. Looking at the reasons you were going after the dream in the first place will help you to see what parts of the dream were non-negotiable and which were just the *fluff* surrounding the essentials. You may find that by redefining the dream, incorporating the key elements and removing the obstacles, it will be able to move on.

The final option is to *go after the dream as you first defined it.* Having carefully looked at the dream again, you decide that despite the challenges, you still believe it is worth going after. So how is it that you regain that initial *fire* to go after the dream in the face of challenges? The key component of keeping motivation alive is in connecting with the heart passion behind your dream. It is easy to get bogged down in the day-to-day grind of having to accomplish tasks and lose sight of the reason you are working so hard. For example, for most of us, there

Today we sailed on.

*Christopher Columbus'
journal entry day after day
during his long voyage
to discover his dream.*

is not much joy in battling the paperwork to obtain a government grant. But when we keep our eyes fixed on the young people that will be affected by the new youth center we are trying to open, it makes it all worthwhile.

Keeping our eyes fixed on the prize is what helps us get through even the toughest times. Jesus said that He kept His eyes fixed on the prize of the joy set before him as He endured the cross. (*See* Hebrews 12:2).

We must learn to do the same.

How will you keep your prize in front of you in the tough

> *The greatest glory in living*
>
> *lies not in never falling,*
>
> *but in rising every time we fall.*
>
> ~ Nelson Mandela

times? Who will help keep you focused on that prize? What does God say about the dream? Answering these questions can help you come up with a plan to keep you motivated before the going even gets tough.

Simple things like putting pictures up as visual cues to remind you of where you are heading can help maintain momentum. Making yourself accountable to a Dream Partner and writing out what God has promised about the dream all help protect the dream from being aborted when the challenging times come. Do whatever you can to keep the passion alive that made the dream worthwhile in the first place.

If your dream is to go to Africa and start an orphanage and you can't get there now, then expose yourself to people who can. Watch DVD's, listen to CD's and read books about people who are doing something similar. It will keep the fire in your belly burning. Stay connected to the passion of what was initially laid in your heart. Review the prophetic words over your life and how they relate to this dream. What has God promised in regard to this? Pray intentionally over the area of passion and ask Him to

continue to breathe on your heart to keep it alive. Write a prayer or declaration concerning the dream; then partner your faith with the declaration and speak words of life into the atmosphere.

cost - the price of pursuing (or not pursuing) a dream

There isn't a dream in the world that hasn't cost the person pursuing it (and quite possibly others around them) at least something. The bigger the dream is, the greater the cost.

So ask yourself, *"What mindset do I need to have in order to proceed when, after starting the journey, the cost looks greater than I actually thought?"* In answering this question, consider the following illustration of a typical shopping experience to buy a new shirt.

As you enter the clothing store, you spot a shirt that you really like. Its color catches your eye and when you look closer you see that the style is exactly what you have been looking for. What is the next thing that most of us do? We look at the price tag. If you are fortunate enough to never have to consider the price of the shirt, then celebrate. But at this point most people look at the cost of the shirt and decide if the shirt is worth that amount of money to them, and whether they can afford it. Maybe you like the shirt enough to pay $20, but you don't like it enough to pay $50. I might like the same shirt enough to pay $70 for it. The point is, we look and consider whether the cost, the investment, or the risk is worth what we are going to get in return. In effect, we ask, *"What is it worth to me personally?"*

To some extent, pursuing a dream is similar. There are things we would like to do, but we have decided that it is not worth the cost to pursue it. For example, I may have a dream of spending three months traveling around Europe and experiencing its history. However, after looking at the *price tag* I reconsider the dream or its timing. The price tag is not only the financial cost, but also the emotional cost of leaving our children behind for that length of time.

For every dream you have, there will be a cost. We see some of the costs up front. When you set out to build a home, you know there are certain costs that you will encounter along the way. The builder will expect to be paid, as will the plumber, electrician and painter. Other costs are not so easily seen, and may sneak up on you unsuspectingly. Many a homebuilder has been ambushed by the unexpected costs for drainage, or some other cost that went beyond budget.

Dreams are like that, too. There are costs that you will see up front and then there are costs that may sneak up on you and test your willingness to proceed. If you own the dream, and the cost is reasonable, you are likely to say, *YES.* But what if the cost is painful? What do you do then?

As in the illustration of purchasing a shirt, you must make a decision whether the dream is worth the cost that is required of you. Now, stop for a moment and have another look at the price tag and consider a different way of viewing the decision to proceed or not.

Let's say your dream is to be a revivalist, and one of the price tags for your dream says: *"Cost = getting up early every day to spend time studying the Bible."* When you encounter the price early in the

morning, it suddenly seems a little high for what you are going to get out of it, at least initially. On the basis of encountering the price tag, you may decide that maybe you aren't really called to be a revivalist. After all, if you were really called to that you would love to get up early and study the Bible.

But before you make a decision not to proceed, consider something else. Flip the price tag over and see that there is another "*cost*" on the back of the tag. This time, it's not the cost of pursuing the dream, but the cost of *not pursuing the dream*. The tag might say, *"Cost of not paying the price = 1,000 souls not saved, 1,500 people not healed, 2,000 people not inspired to pursue Christ with all their being."* When you look at the cost of *not* pursuing becoming the revivalist who God made you to be, getting up early doesn't seem like such a big cost after all.

One of the reasons we have continued to pursue our dream, in spite of what it appears to be costing us up front, is that we are unwilling to pay the price of this dream *not* being fulfilled. Jesus paid in full for us to have access to everything we need to fulfill the dream.

One of my (*Janine's*) dreams is to see every church embrace the truth that women in ministry have as much to offer as men. In the moments when I'm faced with some seemingly insurmountable challenge and consider giving up, I think about my three girls for whom I am the primary female role model. I think about the young women coming behind me who will not be inspired if I don't step up into the fullness of who I am called to be. I think of the dreamers who I am called to inspire who potentially won't pursue their dreams if I don't walk in mine. When I consider the price of *not* pursuing my dream, the cost of advancing somehow shrinks in perspective, and I can do nothing but proceed.

Therefore, when considering the cost of the dream you are about to pursue, don't just look at it at face value. Also consider the cost of *not* pursuing it. Consider Jesus, who for the joy set before Him (that is us!) endured the cross, despising the shame… (*see* Hebrews 12:2).

THE PRICE OF A DREAM

William Wilberforce (1759-1833) was an English revivalist, politician, philanthropist and a leader of the movement to abolish the slave trade.

He was a small, sickly child with poor eyesight, and was plagued with ill health throughout his life. At age 21, Wilberforce spent over £8,000 (*estimated to be equivalent to more than $450,000 USD today*) to purchase a sufficient number of votes to ensure his election as a member of the British Parliament. His intention was just to enjoy this position of influence. However, at age 26, he had a conversion experience resulting in a radical change to his life. He became known as a *"mad Methodist,"* along with the likes of George Whitefield and John Wesley. He gave his life to what he called two *"Divine objects"* —abolish slavery and to make goodness fashionable (*the reformation of morality*).

The first step in abolishing slavery was to make the trading of slaves illegal. The slave trade had involved transporting an estimated 11 million people, of which 1.4 million died during the voyage. Countless others died under the harsh working conditions of the sugar and cotton plantations throughout the British Empire and Colonies.

In spite of Wilberforce's *"divine object"* and an abundance of evidence of the inhumanity of the trade, it took 26 years of persevering until finally the Slave Trade Act of 1807 was passed. This put an end to the trading of slaves but not slavery itself.

Wilberforce had to retire from politics in 1826 due to his failing health, but remained an active supporter of the campaign to completely abolish slavery. In 1833, **three days before Wilberforce died,** the Slavery Abolition Act was passed and it became illegal in the British Empire to own another human being. **After 52 years in pursuit, William Wilberforce finally realized his dream. As a result, the world was forever changed.**

What would have been the cost of not pursuing this dream? After his conversion experience Wilberforce considered retiring from public life to follow a *"call to ministry."* Thankfully two wise friends urged him to stay in parliament and serve Christ there.

What price are you prepared to pay to pursue your dream?

Sources: *Amazing Grace* by Eric Metaxas;
http://en.wikipedia.org/wiki/William_Wilberforce

timing / season change

Life comes in seasons and every season has a different focus. In the natural world, when you think of summer, you think of swimming, barbecues and outdoor fun. Winter brings hot fires, steaming cocoa and adventures in the snow. As it is in the natural world, so it is with dreaming. There are different seasons and we must learn to discern which season we are in and work within that season.

Every season is a season to dream. However, it may be that you don't outwardly pursue that dream in every season. There are seasons when we will actively make concrete, visible action steps toward seeing that dream fulfilled. But there are other seasons when the steps we take to fulfill that dream may be more internal.

For example, if my dream is to be the next Billy Graham, I may see my next step as attending some sort of ministry training school; to start a course of Bible study; or to go on a short term mission trip. These are all outward steps that will move me toward my goal of preparing for the dream. However, there are other seasons that the Lord may also take me through that may not be so easily recognizable as leading me toward my goal. It may be that the Lord takes me through a season of being hidden and learning to rest. In that season I need to know what it is that He is trying to teach me and prepare *in* me so that I can partner with the Holy Spirit.

When the passion and enthusiasm of a dream is high, we want to rush out and do everything we can to move toward the goal. We want to get busy taking the steps that make the dream come

closer, but many times *who we are* is the biggest limiting factor to the dream coming to fruition. We often see money as a limiting factor to achieving our dream. Could it be instead that Heaven is ready to release the finances when we are ready to face the limitations of unbelief, negativity or poor character inside of us? I'm not saying we need to be perfect to begin to chase a dream, but I am saying we need to give as much attention to the internal requirements as we do to the external ones.

Learning to discern the season you are in by listening to the voice of the Lord is an essential tool for a Dreamer. In Scripture, there were seasons when the Israelites had to go to battle, and seasons when the Lord simply gave them the victory if they so much as showed up to fight. Their job was to inquire of the Lord and find out what their part was for each battle.

The same is true for you and me. We must go to the Lord and find out what is our part in making the dream come true. Does the Lord want you to save diligently to attend your college classes, or is He going to provide supernaturally through a sponsor? Are you in a time of pushing into prayer in a strong way, or is it a season of God teaching you to rest and letting Him fight your battle? Knowing the answers to these questions is essential in moving toward your dream.

We must be a people who know how to partner with the Holy Spirit in pursuit of becoming who we are called to be. A healthy partnership requires that each partner knows what their part is and that they do their share. Failure to do your part, or expecting God to do it all, will result in the dream being stillborn. But trying to do God's part will also damage the dream. Hearing His voice is what allows us to partner with Him and see what He wants birthed on the earth.

One final word on seasons: there will be seasons where it is okay *not* to focus entirely on your dreams. Once again, it is about hearing the voice of the Lord and responding to it.

Maybe you have just moved to a new city or country. Maybe a close relative has just died or you are having a new baby. Maybe you have started a new job or ministry. All these things require a tremendous amount of emotional energy from you as you adjust to your new circumstances. It may be that, while you are in this season, you put the pursuit of dreams aside for a time. This is all right, but be sure that the season doesn't last a lifetime. We have seen how easy it is for young mothers in particular to put their dreams on hold while they have their babies. They wake up 10 or 20 years later only to realize that they neglected to pick up their dreams again. The tragedy is that many of them have so lost touch with their dreams that they find it hard even to remember what they were.

If you have an extended period where you are unable, for whatever reason, to pursue your dreams, we encourage you to do something to keep the dream alive by continuing to work on who you need to *be* in order to walk out the dream.

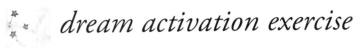

dream activation exercise

step one | **Owning Your Dream**

So how do you know if you truly own your dream? Take some time to consider one of your dreams and then answer the following questions:

— How ready are you to commit energy, time and resources to pursue this dream?

— If no one else joins or supports you, will you still pursue it?

— What would it take for you to let it go or replace it?

— How important or relevant is this dream to you?

— How responsible do you feel to bring this dream to pass?

— What have you done to demonstrate you own this dream? Is it written down? Who else knows about it? What price have you paid so far? What opposition have you already overcome?

— Now that you have answered these questions, do you really own this dream, or is it someone else's expectation of you?

step two | **Tapping the Passion - The Motivation of a Dream**

Keeping our heart connected to the passion and our eyes fixed on the prize is what helps us get through even the toughest times in the pursuit of a dream. Discover the passion behind your dreams and the prize you look forward to by asking yourself the following questions. You may choose to do this with a Dream Friend and even record or journal your responses.

— What inspired the dream in the first place? What is behind it?

— How is it a reflection of your values, attitudes and passions?

— What does God say about this dream?

— Imagine yourself living this dream sometime in the future. Now describe in detail what it would look like, feel like, taste like? What would be the effect of this happening in your life? How would this effect the lives of others?

— How will you keep your prize in front of you in the tough times? Who will help keep you focused on that prize?

— How motivated are you to go after this dream now? Rate it on a scale of one to ten, where a one is, "Who cares?" and a ten is, "I would give my life for this." What would need to happen for this level of motivation to increase?

step three | **Counting the Cost**

For every dream you have, there will be a cost. Some costs are easily seen. Other costs are not so easily seen, and may sneak up on you unsuspectingly.

— What could be the cost of achieving your dream? Money? Time? Relationships? Attitudes and beliefs? Are there other physical or emotional costs?

— What is the cost of not pursuing this dream? In your life? In the lives of those around you? In the lives of those following you? In the lives of those yet to be born?

— Is this dream worth the cost?

— What would need to change for it to be worth the cost?

step four | **Knowing the Season and Timing**

Every season is a season to dream. However, it may be that you don't outwardly pursue a particular dream in every season. The key to knowing, is listening to the voice of God – His Spirit, His Word and His wise counselors that He placed around your life.

— What is the Holy Spirit speaking to you in regard to how hard you pursue your dream in this season? What should you be doing? What does He want to do for you? Ask or write down the question, then pause to hear with your heart what He says.

— Who are the wise counselors that God has placed around your life at this time? A parent? A pastor or leader? A boss? How could you access the wisdom they may have for you at this time?

— Is this the time to pursue your dream externally, or prepare internally, or both? How ready are you internally (character, attitude, beliefs) for this dream to be realized?

— If this is not the season to fully pursue your dreams, what things could you do to keep the passion and dream alive?

overcoming speed bumps

Yet in all these things we are more than conquerors...

Romans 8:37

In order to be called overcomers, we must first overcome something. In order to become *more than* overcomers, we must overcome *well!* Challenges are not a sign that you are going the wrong way or have made the wrong choice; they may well just be the perfect preparation for you to be able to handle the dream when it is fully realized.

what if i get stuck?

When we initially tap into our dream, there is a release of life, initiative and momentum that gets us moving toward it. The excitement of this discovery compels us to move forward. Remember when you first encountered Jesus or first met the man or woman of your dreams? Nothing could stop you from

talking about it and doing everything you could to grow the relationship. However, as you began the journey, you started to come across speed bumps, challenges and mindsets that were resistant to progress.

In this section, we'll cover a few of the restraints that we have encountered the most. Our intent is to expose these up front so you're prepared, making the speed bump an opportunity to strengthen you rather than something that stops you.

Proverbs says, *"Hope deferred makes the heart sick, but when the desire comes it is a tree of life"* (Proverbs 13:12). Most of us who have lived very long have felt the disappointment of a dream unfulfilled. Most of us have experienced what it is like to dream a dream and not have it work out like we expected. When it doesn't work out like we thought it would we question whether the dream was really legitimate or from God in the first place. We think that if it were from God, it would come together easily. And when it looks like a failure, we abandon it as just *our* idea.

> *I am not afraid...*
> *I was born to do this.*
> - Joan of Arc

We feel ashamed of the failure of not living the dream and of even thinking we could ever live it, so we kill the dream and convince ourselves that it was not from God. We keep a row of coffins containing lost dreams lined up on the inside of us. Every time we start to dream again, we look inside our hearts and see that line-up reminding us of all the dreams that didn't come true. Those coffins are a powerful reminder of all the reasons we shouldn't go after the new dream. They remind us of our failures and of

God's apparent disregard for our dream. They prompt questions like: *Why should I dream again? Why will it be different this time?*

If we are to pursue the dream of becoming all we are called to be, we must find a way to silence the voices coming from the coffins of the dreams yet unfulfilled. Doing this means pulling the coffins into the light. Our natural instinct is to hide the dead thing and never look at it again. We believe we can move on with our lives and ignore what didn't work. Instead, we need to open up the coffins and take a good look at the dreams that still lie inside. Some dreams that lie dead are the result of bad choices that we made. Some died because of other peoples' choices. Some died simply of neglect. Some died on the battlefield after a valiant attempt at reaching them failed. The thing they all have in common is they are dead and they serve to remind us that dreams don't always come true.

The problem with letting them lie dormant in your heart is that they echo lies to you and try to tell you no dreams will ever come true for you. Whenever you try to get up and dream again, they scream: *Don't dream. It's not worth the pain. Don't you remember what happened last time?* The ghosts of dead dreams taunt you with the memory of your past failures. Their aim is to get you so entwined with the fear of the past that you will not move forward and seize your future.

> *God, who gives life to the dead and calls those things which do not exist as though they did.*
>
> Romans 4:17b

It's time to silence the voice of these dead dreams and let the voice

of the Dream Giver speak again! It's time to have a discussion with Him over the contents of the coffins, to hear what He has to say about them. We're sure you will discover that He has a different perspective of the *ugly old bones* that you would rather hide in shame.

I love the story of the valley of dry bones in Ezekiel 37. Bones that are dried out have been dead a long time. You and I would generally look at something dead that long as being past hope, even for God. Yet God saw, even in the desiccated bones, an opportunity for new life. And the good news is He wants to do the same for you. He wants to bring resurrection power to the dead dreams inside of you.

It is time to silence the voice of the dead dreams and let the voice of the Dream Giver speak again!

Just as God did in the valley of the dry bones, He wants to breathe life into something that looks beyond hope. Life came back into the bones by the Word of God being spoken over them. It's time to speak over your dreams and put muscles and tendons back on them. It's time to call forth the winds of the Spirit to breathe fresh life into the dreams and call for them to live again. The dreams may look different than when they died, but that's all right. When God resurrects something, He never brings it back worse than it started. He brings it back to life better than before.

Your dreams are powerful. God has a potent weapon in His hands to use in His quest to transform the world. That weapon is you and your dream. When you live in pursuit of Him and of becoming all He has called you to be, you are going to come against opposition. The enemy is not happy about you becoming an agent of change in the earth. He doesn't want you representing the Father in all His fullness, so opposition is to be expected.

We must become adept at seeing the enemy's strategies to turn us off course and become skilled at overcoming them. Romans 8:37 says we are *more* than conquerors. For this to

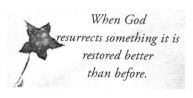

When God resurrects something it is restored better than before.

become reality in our lives we need to have something that we have conquered. The fantastic thing is, it is through Christ that we have victory. In Him we find love, hope, faith, strength and every other resource we need, not just to survive, but also to valiantly conquer!

Remember that our enemy's lies and tricks only have power if we come into agreement with them. He will try to discourage you, disillusion you and disappoint you. These things only have the power to derail you if you let them. The good news is that God has given us the answer to these tricks.

DREAMS RESURRECTED
& LIFE RELEASED

Janet had a love for painting early in life and can remember as a young child getting art lessons at great expense to the family. But somewhere along the journey, her love of being creative was stifled. Now, at age 63, she began to dream again and meet with a Dream Coach. As she did, Janet realized that she had some fear associated with painting and being creative, but making a decision to push past the fear enabled her to set some daily action steps to rediscover her creative side. Breakthrough came when the Holy Spirit brought a revelation to her that she truly had permission to be on a creative journey with Him. She didn't have to have all the answers and could make mistakes along the way.

Since then, Janet has begun a new journey of creativity. She has a new lease on life, creating for craft shows and producing all sorts of arts and crafts. She also shares that love with older people in the community, encouraging them to explore their creative side. Even more, her art is being used by God to release His Presence. Janet created a picture inspired by her encounter with the Lord when He gave her permission to dream. She took the painting to a friend who was feeling overwhelmed by the pressures of life. The friend was set free from discouragement! God resurrected a childhood dream to paint, and now Janet and those around her are experiencing life flowing through her in a new way.

regaining courage

The antidote to *dis-couragement* is courage. We need courage to run at the battle; courage to pursue the dream when you don't see the solutions to the problems that you need solved; courage to pursue the dream no matter what you feel. If you are low on courage then ask someone to lend you theirs until yours is strengthened again. Encouragement is the giving or lending of one's courage to another. It is one of the greatest gifts we can give the people around us and so greatly needed all the time.

King David learned to encourage himself in the Lord and you can do the same. A great resource to help build strength in this area is Bill Johnson's book, *Strengthen Yourself in the Lord*.

restoring hope

The antidote to *dis-illusionment* is illumination. Disillusionment comes when we lose sight of the dream or goal due to the multitude of challenges directly in front, or even surrounding us. If you feel disillusioned, then seek to get more of His light on the situation; get insight on how Heaven sees the issue at hand. We are seated in heavenly places with Christ. The view from the Throne is quite different than from here in the midst of the trials. Heaven is not concerned over lack of money or power. It is not concerned about your lack of adequacy. When we get illuminated on Heaven's perspective and come into agreement with that, disillusionment can't operate. One encounter with Heaven restores hope and the ability to see again. Strengthen your connection with the Father and with people who carry His presence. Remind yourself of how far He has brought you, and of His promises for your future. Listen to the prophetic words over your life again and remember what He has done on your behalf in the past.

Recently, I had a number of experiences that on their own would have been easy to overcome, but together they took my eyes off my dream. It took a couple of days to figure out what had even happened. During that time, I took a number of recent prophetic words that had been recorded and some key chapters of Psalms that were significant to me and put them onto my iPod. I then spent most of a day with one ear listening over and over to the promises as I went about my weekend chores. I could feel hope rising within me as I was reminded of what God had said and I again encountered His Presence. I am now armed and regularly listen to my prophetic words or the Psalms to keep my soul flooded with hope.

One encounter with Heaven restores hope...

overcoming disappointment

The remedy to *dis-appointment* is to remember that you are appointed! Disappointment comes when things don't work out how we expect them to. Disappointment actually means *to remove from office*. Missed expectation can knock us off course or off the journey that we were appointed to pursue. In those moments, we tend to focus on how things *should* have been and how they didn't turn out the way we expected. Focus instead on the fact that God appointed you for such a time as this. Let your gaze focus on His ability to turn circumstances into the right ones that set you up for success.

When your gaze is filled with His love for you and His appointment of you for the task, you will take the disappointment that tries to knock you off course in your stride. Again, we cannot overemphasize the value and strength we gain by having Dream Partners or Dream Friends around us that continually remind us of who we really are and call us higher into life.

Life flows from connection. Remember, God can and does turn the things that seem to be a mess or disappointment into stepping stones for greatness. You are loved by God and called according to His purpose, so it's impossible for Him *not* to work your failures into something good! Hand Him your disappointment and wait expectantly for what He will give you in return.

dream activation exercise

God's Dream For Me...

step one | **Reflect**

You dream because you were made in the image of the most audacious Dreamer there is: God. He dreamed the whole universe up – and it came to be. And before you were born, He dreamed of you.

What is God's dream for you? Take some time to meditate on these questions and ask what the Holy Spirit wants to show you about God's dream for you:

— God sees the best you, the you He created. What do you look like to Him?

— What is the picture God has in His mind of who you were made to be?

— What is God's dream for His relationship with you? What does He long for and look forward to for you?

— When God pictures His dream for you, how does it make Him feel?

step two | **Reinforce**

Do this Dream Activation with your Dream Friend or Dream Partner. Have each person in turn share what they saw as God's dream for them. As you listen, tune in to what the Holy Spirit would add to that dream. What else is in God's heart for this person? Take time to pray, prophecy and affirm each other.

step three | **Face the Voices of the Past**

Become aware of the voices that discourage you from pursuing your dreams. These are the things that you hear when you are at a critical junctures in pursuit of your dream. Instead of trying to ignore the voices:

— Pull them to the surface. What am I really thinking?

— Examine the thoughts in the light of the truth. Is this truth speaking to me or is it a lie? What does Jesus have to say about this? Ask the Holy Spirit to reveal the truth to you. If you are unsure.

— Ask a faith filled friend to help you see the truth.

— Choose to believe what God says about you rather than what your past experience tries to tell you.

— Declare the truth over yourself. For example: God is good and He is for my dreams. He has placed dreams in me and will release Heaven's resources to see them lived out. If you have had a series of disappointments then you will need to continue to choose to believe truth and dislodge old lies until new truth becomes revelation to you.

— Make a plan for living unstoppable. What could you do to keep the truth about you and your dreams

in front of you? What plan do you have for the next time your dreams are challenged? What tools can you arm yourself with so that you are set up to overcome?

overcoming mindsets

Set your mind on things above, not on things on the earth.

Colossians 3:2

Three common mindsets we have experienced that keep many potential Dreamers from pursuing their dreams are The Servant Mindset, The Hamster Mindset and The Lottery Mindset. These mindsets are common and on the surface may even appear Biblical.

The most effective lie is one that has enough truth in it to be believable. Each of these mindsets has enough Biblical truth to be believed, but each is twisted by the enemy to become a trap that stops us from becoming all that we are called to be. As the apostle Peter exhorted: *Be sober, be vigilant* of the enemy's tricks (*see* I Peter 5:8). But never forget, greater is He that is in you than He that is in the world (*see* I John 4:4); and we are seated with Christ in Heavenly realms! (*See* Ephesians 2:6). Mindsets are not a problem as long as our mind is set on the right thing:

Set your mind on things above,
not on things on the earth.

Colossians 3:2

Two great resources for building right mindsets are Steve Backlund's books *Cracks in the Foundation* and *Victorious Mindsets*. These are written in such a way that you can use them to help build heavenly mindsets on a daily basis.

servant mindset

The Servant Mindset is a very popular mindset in the Church. We have heard much teaching on being a servant. After all, Jesus is our model and He came to serve and not to be served. But Scripture also talks about how we progress from being servants to becoming friends. *"No longer do I call you servants…but I have called you friends…"* (*see* John 15:15). The difference between a servant and a friend in this context is *knowing* the will of God compared to *being told* what to do. The difference is relationship and personal revelation.

We have encountered many people who are constrained by a Servant Mindset that stops them from pursuing who they are. They are in servant mode so much that they have given up thinking for themselves and they now just want to be told what to do.

Jesus has given us gifts, passions and abilities that He wants us to pursue in order to show His glory on the earth. Laying all your dreams aside in order to serve may seem very noble, but does it serve Heaven's purpose on the earth? Our greatest contributions come as we serve, yet continue to dream.

It's time for believers to grow up and take their place as *friends of God,* knowing who and what they are called to be, rather than nobly serving in a role that doesn't fit them.

As previously stated, there are different seasons in life and some of those seasons will involve service in an area where your passions and gifts may not be utilized. A commitment to follow your dreams does not equate to an excuse not to serve in the Body. That being said, as we grow into mature believers, we should be looking to serve in a way that allows for our gifts and passions to have their greatest expression. When we serve where our passions lie, instead of out of a sense of duty, we are much more likely to go the distance. Jesus is returning to marry a Bride, not a slave!

hamster mindset

Have you ever had a hamster in the house? Our family has one named Buddy that belongs to our daughter, Emily. He has long whiskers, a twitchy nose and lovely soft fur with beautiful markings. In short, he is cute! But, and this is a big deal, he runs *all night long* on his hamster wheel.

At first this was also very cute. Our three-year-old would call out, *"Buddy is on the wheel,"* and the whole family would gather around and watch Buddy run. However, after a couple of weeks, it was no longer cute or fun to watch Buddy run.

It is, however, fascinating to watch how night after night a small

animal can expend so much energy on going nowhere. You and I are much smarter than a hamster. We would only do something so mindless and so obviously unproductive if we were intentionally doing it to lose weight or to stay fit, right?

Well, we would hope so, but watching Buddy on the wheel night after night reminds us of some of the Dreamers we have met. These people are very busy running on their wheel of life. Day after day they get very busy; too busy to stop and think; too busy to stop and evaluate life; too busy to dream.

You have to decide what your highest priorities are and have the courage - pleasantly, smilingly, non-apologetically - to say "no" to other things.
And the way you do that is by having a bigger "yes" burning inside. The enemy of the "best" is often the "good."
- Stephen Covey

One day I suspect that these people will fall off their wheel in exhaustion and hopefully take time to think before they jump back on. My prayer is that they will take time to ask if they are on the right wheel. I pray that they will check if God wants them to be running that hard without apparently getting very far.

The Hamster Mindset comes from a belief that being busy for God is the same as being productive for God. You will produce the most fruit for the Kingdom when you are serving in the sphere in which you were designed to serve, and sometimes you have to slow down long enough to discover what that is. Even when we do discover what God is calling us to, we must keep enough room in our schedules to consciously invest time in pursuing the greater things that God has for us—our dreams! The only person that has complete responsibility and authority over your time is you (*unless you are under the care of a guardian or prison officer*). Busyness is part of the curse. Jesus broke the curse so that everything we do would come out of rest, out of peace, out of connection with Him and with others. That doesn't mean that my schedule is not full, but rather that my schedule is arranged around my priorities and my purpose.

What things are you doing that are not actually going anywhere? What does your life say about your priorities? When did you last stop to review how you are spending your time and how effective that is? Why are you doing what you are doing? We challenge you to recheck your priorities, your schedule and your productivity. It is time to get off that hamster wheel, and make your dreams a reality.

lottery mindset

The other major mindset that we see in Dreamers we work with is the Lottery Mindset. These people think that at any moment their Daddy in the sky will suddenly and unexpectedly drop their dream, in its entirety, into their lap. They look at the stories in the Bible where the *"hero"* comes into an *"and suddenly"* moment and everything seems to change overnight. The result is that they do nothing in the meantime. *"That will be me,"* they figure, *"if I just stay in faith and believe God."*

This may be true with a few dreams, but our experience is that it takes both faith *and* action to become who God has made

you to be. What you often don't see, unless you take the time to look hard, is that most *"and suddenly"* moments in the Bible have an unseen component in them. The reality is that most of the time it takes many years and a lot of hard work to become an overnight success. What you do in the years while you are waiting for your *"and suddenly"* moment to come will determine whether it actually comes or not.

As James says, *"...faith without works is dead ... show me your faith without your works and I will show you my faith by my works"* (see James 2:18,26). Even Jesus said, *"If I do not do the works of my Father, do not believe me"* (see John 10:37). Unless my actions are lining up with what I'm saying, don't believe me. So unless you are actually making some conscious steps toward your dream, maybe it's just a dead dream or a dream not worth believing in.

...most of the time it takes many years and a lot of hard work to become an overnight success.

Bill Johnson likes to say, *"Most of what you need will come to you, but most of what you want you will have to go after."* You are the one who is responsible to go after becoming who God has made you to be, and it will take concentrated effort to stay on course. You are powerful. God will not do for you what you can do for yourself. That would not be a partnership and would actually disempower you. God is teaching us how to partner with Heaven by starting with what is in our hand and then seeing the impossible *suddenly* happen.

A few years ago, I was a part of a team that was responsible for creating a church preschool. It was a massive undertaking. We did a building renovation worth $100,000, a playground renovation worth $50,000 and we had to coordinate with government agencies including the fire department

If you do nothing,
nothing
gets done.

and building inspectors, as well as volunteers who helped with the actual work. All this took place over the Christmas summer holidays in New Zealand, when almost all service providers shut down for up to three weeks.

I learned a lot through being involved with this process, and the biggest lesson was this: *If you do nothing, nothing gets done.* In order for our preschool to open on time, we needed courage, faith and just plain hard work. If we had stopped with courage and faith, the preschool would not have opened. But as we partnered our faith in God's goodness with our hard work, we saw miracles take place and the preschool opened on time for the New Year, despite all those who said it couldn't be done. What do you need to do today to walk towards your dream? Do you know what your part is and what part belongs to God? Now is the time to find out, because when you do your part, God will surely do His.

dream activation exercise

step one | **What is Your Mind Set On?**

As you read through this section, what thoughts, feelings or revelations did you notice or become aware of in yourself?

— What do those feelings tell you about what you believe?

— If you were on the outside observing the way you live, what mindsets would you see evidenced?

— What would you like to do about that?

As with chapter five about beliefs, the way to establish mindsets built on truth is to first connect with the Spirit of Truth.

If then you were raised with Christ, seek those things which are above,
where Christ is, sitting at the right hand of God.
Set your mind on things above, not on things on the earth.
For you died, and your life is hidden with Christ in God.

Colossians 3:1-3

Take some time to connect with the Father, meditating on the above Scripture and then ask the following questions:

— What does it look or feel like to be hidden with Christ in God?

— Who are the Father and the Son to you?

— Who are you to the Father and the Son? A servant? A friend? A beloved companion?

— What is the Holy Spirit saying to you about who you are and who you were made to be?

— Which nature or aspect of Heaven is it that you want to set your mind on?

— What aspect of the nature of Christ do you most admire and resonate with? What do you bring to the earth?

step two | **Living As a Friend of God** (antidote to a Servant Mindset)

You are a powerful decision maker designed to co-create with Heaven.

— How can you establish a mindset of being a friend of God (with a serving heart) rather than a servant waiting for the next instructions?

— What has God given you to display through your life on the earth?

— What do your dreams say about what your life message or life purpose may be? What is in your heart to do?

— What does your Father want to co—create on the earth with you?

— What has He been saying to you personally?

— Take a moment to reflect on what you are hearing God say and write it down. Now ask yourself what one thing you will do differently this week to move forward and live your dreams as God intended?

step three | **Protecting the Priorities** (antidote to a Hamster Mindset)

If you don't protect what is important to you, no one else will.

— What does your schedule say about what is important to you? What are your priorities based on your daily or weekly activities?

— If you asked a friend or workmate, what would they say is most important to you?

— How much time do you spend on activities where you come away thinking, "That was a waste of time."

— What could you do about that?

Consider doing the following activities to build a life of living intentionally, of living from purpose:

— First, make a list of the top five to ten roles or priorities in your life. Consider roles such as being a friend of God, a husband or wife, a parent, a friend, a son or daughter, and a leader in the area specific to your life and calling.

— How would you like to be known in each of these key roles?

— What would you like to have said at your funeral?

— Now that you have identified your key roles and what you want to be known for, design a one or two sentence statement that captures this. For example, Andy has a priority of being a "Great Husband." His statement defining this priority looks like this: "Janine will say of me, 'He is my devoted companion and greatest champion. He lives as Christ to me in loving me into fullness of life. Together we establish a heavenly model of what a godly couple in ministry and life look like.'"

Now consider what you could do to make those written priorities an actual priority evidenced in your life.

— What could you do to remind yourself daily or weekly about what is most important to you?

— Who could you share your priorities with to help you keep accountable to your plan?

— How could you build your priorities into your week?

— How are you going to protect time in your schedule for the pursuit of your dreams?

step four | **Living Powerfully** (antidote to a Lottery Mindset)

Living powerfully is about taking responsibility for what is yours to do. It is about focusing on what you can do and not on what you cannot do. In considering your dreams think about the following:

— What are the things that are already in your hand that you could do something about now?

— How could you prepare, propel or position yourself to be ready for when the next door to your dream opens?

— If you imagined one of your friends giving you advice about your dream, what do you think he or she would say about where you should start?

— What could you do that you are not currently doing?

— Ask the Holy Spirit to open your eyes to see what He has already placed in your hand, what is already within your reach or is accessible through the relationships around you?

See Matthew 14:15 – 21

— In this partnership of moving forward in your dreams, ask the Holy Spirit what He will do and what you need to do.

now coach yourself and others

Freely you have received, freely give.

Matthew 10:8b

Our expectation is that in reading this book and working through the activation exercises you have put legs on your dreams, and also acquired tools to coach yourself as you move forward. Beyond that, our prayer is that you will also use these tools every day among the people around you to help build a culture that inspires and empowers people in the fulfillment of their dreams.

We want to experience the joy of all creation coming fully alive. In order for this to happen, we must help each other dream bigger and walk out the fulfillment of those dreams.

so where to from here?

In summarizing some key points from this book, we encourage you to invest in the following:

ONE
dream bigger and start with what's in your hand

Make it a daily habit to follow through on simple decisions and actions that move you toward your dream. You will be amazed how "suddenly" you are living many of your dreams. Consider getting yourself a Dream Journal or starting a blog to record your adventures. Maybe you could even put pictures of your dreams in conspicuous places where you will bump into them as you walk through life – in the pages of your favorite book or magazine, over the bathroom mirror, on the refrigerator door, or even on the dashboard of your car. Release the creativity you were born with, dream bigger and live louder!

TWO
find a dream friend or dream partner

Build a relationship with someone who can become a Dream Friend or Dream Partner and who will help keep you encouraged and accountable in the pursuit and fulfillment of your dreams. Maybe you could even do this for each other. Look for someone who will love you enough to ask the hard questions. Find a friend who will not allow their own disappointments, fears or limitations to spill out on you and quench your dreams, but instead will pour more fuel on your fire. You need to both hear and speak encouraging comments and questions like these:

- "Wow that dream is amazing!"
- "How are you getting on with your dreams?"
- "What steps have you made this week to move toward those dreams becoming reality?"
- "What is stopping you from moving forward on that dream?"
- "When was the last time you sat down to dream again... bigger!"

THREE
find someone YOU can encourage in the pursuit of their dreams

Freely you have received, now freely give. You have a testimony that will unlock and unleash the lives of others. Just being around somebody who is experiencing life more abundantly is a contagious experience. People everywhere are just waiting for someone to believe in them. You have what it takes. Every day we literally bump into people who need encouragement like a baby needs food. Without it, life becomes stunted and empty of energy and fun. Who will you bump into today, intentionally or not? Who could you encourage in their dreams? It is amazing how even a smile can encourage someone's day.

FOUR
develop a toolbox of questions

Develop your toolbox of questioning skills and also your listening ears. But even more importantly, listen to the One who asks the most powerful questions—the Holy Spirit.

- "I believe in you! What is your dream?"
- "What five things can you do now to start moving toward that dream?"
- "What will you do?"
- "When do you plan on completing that?"
- "What do you already have in your hand that you can use to start?"
- "How can I help keep you on track?"

Our purpose above and beyond any program or book is that together we will create a culture where everyone is intentionally looking to help one another's dreams become reality.

You now hold the baton. What will you do with it?

If you would like further information, please contact us at **www.idreamculture.com.** We would love to hear testimonies of dreams coming true and Dreamers being inspired and empowered on their Dream Journey. Thanks for partnering with us to develop a Global Dream Culture… as it is in Heaven. Together we can change the world, one Dreamer at a time!

If God is your God, dream bigger…
then start with what is in your hand.

DREAM RESOURCES

dream starters

One way to unlock more dreams is to write down at least one dream for each of the questions below. If you are a natural dreamer, that is, you easily envision the future even when you don't know how to get there, use the first set of questions. If you are a practical person and have a hard time detaching yourself from "*what is*" to think about "*what could be*," try the list on the following page.

- What gives you pleasure?
- What is beautiful for you?
- What do you want to do just for fun?
- If you were fearless, what would you try?
- What do you value most in the world?
- What do you need?
- What needs of others tug at your heart?
- Who do you dream for, and what is your dream for them?
- If you could change one thing in the world, what would it be?
- What would Heaven on earth look like to you?
- What do you dream will happen when you get to Heaven?
- Who do you know that is living their dream? What do you love about their life?
- What thought or idea have you had that you haven't

acted on? Maybe you thought it was too big, foolish, or inconsequential to name as a dream.

- What would make your spiritual life really soar? Your emotional life? Your physical life?

- What would you do if money were no limitation?

more dream starters

- What in your life now gives you pleasure? Which of those things could you do more of?

- Where have you seen beauty in life? Which of these things would you like to have in your life now?

- What do you do for fun, when you really cut loose or aren't worried so much about what it costs?

- What is the most fearless thing you have done? What else would you try if you felt like that?

- What do you value most in the world? How could that increase?

- What do you need? What would it look like if that need was filled? What needs of others tug at your heart?

- Who do you know that you wish had a better life? What would you do for them if you could?

- If you could change one thing in the world, what would it be?

- Where have you most clearly seen Heaven on earth? Would you like more of that?

- What do you dream will happen to you when you get to Heaven?

- Who do you know is living their dream? What do

you love about their life?

- What thought or idea have you had that you haven't acted on? Maybe you thought it was too big or foolish or inconsequential to name as a dream.

- What makes your spiritual life really soar? Your emotional life? Your physical life?

additional ideas to get you thinking...

What thoughts and dreams do the following examples trigger in you?

Professional dreams - Be the top salesperson for the year; Gain national accreditation.

Family dreams - Get married; Be the best father I can be.

Financial dreams - Pay off all credit cards; Grow five sources of income.

Creative dreams - Paint a mural in a public place; Write a song for my children.

Places to visit - The Great Wall of China; The place where my grandparents were born.

Skills to master - Gourmet BBQ; A golf handicap of less than 10.

Books to read - The Bible from cover to cover; One book every month.

Events to attend - A U2 concert; Fourth of July in New York.

Subjects to research - The history of America; Divine health.

Things you've always wanted to do - Bungee jump; Spend the night in a mud hut.

Subjects you want to study - Gravity; History; Spanish.

Places you want to visit - The Great Pyramids; Dunkirk; New Zealand.

Experiences you want to have - Hot air balloon ride; Scuba dive off the Great Barrier Reef.

Cultural food experiences - Eat a seven-course gourmet meal; Attend a medieval birthday party.

People you want to meet - Bono; Muhammad Yunus; President of a country.

Countries you want to visit - Russia; Turkey; Tahiti; Israel; the "newest" and "oldest."

Hobbies you want to have - Model plane building; Cake decorating; Golf.

Kind of spouse you want to have - Lover of Jesus; Creative; Wise.

Children and grandchildren you want to have - Smarter than me; Go further and faster.

Things you want to have - An income while I sleep; A house; A yellow Chevy Camaro with black stripes.

Things you want to buy - A digital camera; A world trip for my wife; A house.

Sports you want to try - American football; Lacrosse; Cross-country skiing.

Physical condition you want to be in - Less than 200 pounds; Able to run five miles at any time.

How you would like to look - Sharp and confident, but relaxed and friendly.

Feelings you want to feel - Euphoria of conquering a mountain; Overwhelmed by love.

Gifts you want to give - A house to a pastor in Africa; A million dollars at one time.

The kind of lifestyle you want to have - 30 hours a week "working" and more time with children.

The friends you want to have - A president; A homeless man; A Muslim cleric.

The way you want to spend time with friends - Adventures outdoors; Living their dreams.

The relationship you want to have with your family - Powerful, free and happy.

The financial freedom you want to be in - Leave an inheritance for my children's children.

The toys you would want to buy yourself – Remote control off-road car; Model railway; crossbow.

The charity you want to contribute to - My own; World Vision; Opportunity International.

The thing you want to be remembered for - Love; empowering others; Miracles.

RECOMMENDED READING

A Leader's Life Purpose Workbook by Tony Stoltzfus.
www.coach22.com, 2009.

Coaching Questions by Tony Stoltzfus.
www.coach22.com, 2008.

Cracks in the Foundation by Steve Backlund.
www.ignitedhope.com, 2007.

Dream Manager by Matthew Kelly.
Beacon Publishing, 2007.

Face to Face With God by Bill Johnson.
Destiny Image, 2007.

Put Your Dream to the Test by John C. Maxwell.
Thomas Nelson, 2009.

Strengthen Yourself in the Lord by Bill Johnson.
Destiny Image, 2007.

The Dream Giver by Bruce Wilkinson.
Multnomah Publishers, 2003.

The Seven Habits of Highly Effective People by Stephen R. Covey.
Simon and Schuster, 1990.

Victorious Mindsets by Steve Backlund.
www.ignitedhope.com, 2008.

REFERENCES

Amazing Grace – William Wilberforce and the Heroic Campaign to End Slavery
by Eric Metaxas. Harper Collins, 2007.

Coaching Questions: A Coach's Guide to Powerful Asking Skills
by Tony Stoltzfus. www.coach22.com, 2008.

Leadership Coaching: The Disciplines, Skills and Heart of a Christian Coach
by Tony Stoltzfus. www.coach22.com, 2005.

Put Your Dream to the Test: 10 Questions to Help You See It and Seize It
by John Maxwell. Thomas Nelson, 2009.

The Element: How Finding Your Passion Changes Everything
by Dr. Ken Robinson. Penguin Books, 2009.

http://en.wikipedia.org/ and http://wiki.answers.com/

ABOUT THE AUTHORS

Andy and Janine Mason come from the beautiful east coast of New Zealand. Together with their four elementary aged children and ten suitcases, they arrived in Redding, California in August of 2008. They had a dream to give their lives to develop people. Little did they know that they would soon be partnering with Danny Silk and his new team at Bethel Church helping build an organization to build the lives of people. Andy and Janine are directors of Bethel's Dream Culture program and part of the leadership team for Global Transformation Institute.

Dream Culture, launched in early 2010, is a ministry that encourages and empowers people to discover their dreams and make practical steps to live out their purpose. What began at Bethel Church is now catalyzing dreamers and Dream Cultures in schools, businesses, churches and community groups around the world.

Their six session *Dream Journey Workshop* is now available on DVD with a companion workbook.

Before coming to Redding, Andy worked for a leading financial institution and a national consultancy firm. His primary role was helping clients define what success was to them, then partnering with them in developing strategic plans towards realizing that success. Andy was also involved for ten years in the leadership team of a local church in New Zealand. Janine's background is in people development, adult training and project management, for both non-profit and profit-based organizations. In addition to being a wonderful mother to four children, Janine is known for her perceptive questions that quickly help clients get to the heart of the matter and develop practical and holistic approaches for moving forward.

Dream Culture, Bringing Dreams to Life is also available in Spanish and German.

For more information visit: www.iDreamCulture.com